CRITICAL READING SERIES

DECEPTIONS

21 Fascinating Stories of Trickery and Fraud—with Exercises for Developing Reading Comprehension and Critical Thinking Skills

Henry Billings

Melissa Billings

JAMESTOWN PUBLISHERS

a division of NTC/CONTEMPORARY PUBLISHING GROUP
Lincolnwood, Illinois USA

ISBN 0-89061-113-0

Published by Jamestown Publishers,
a division of NTC/Contemporary Publishing Group, Inc.
4255 West Touhy Avenue,
Lincolnwood (Chicago), Illinois 60712-1975, U.S.A.
© 1999 NTC/Contemporary Publishing Group, Inc.

4 5 6 7 8 9 10 11 12 13 14 113 09 08 07 06 05 04 03 02

CONTENTS

UNIT THREE

To the Student

A s little children, we are all taught not to tell lies. Honesty, we are told, is the best policy. The people you will read about in this book did not take this childhood advice to heart. Instead, they practiced deception. Some of them fell into trickery or fraud just once in a moment of weakness. Others depended upon it throughout their lives.

Each lesson will introduce you to a different person or group of people who chose to lie to get what they wanted. Often their lives ended in unhappiness or even disaster as a result of their dishonesty. You will learn about acts of deception that are sometimes clever, often criminal, occasionally amusing (especially if you are not the victim of the trickery), but always gripping.

Almost all the articles tell about actual events recorded in books and newspapers. As you read and enjoy them, you will also be developing your reading skills. *Deceptions* is for students who already read fairly well but who want to read faster and to increase their understanding of what they read. If you complete the 21 lessons—reading the articles and completing the exercises—you will surely increase your reading speed and improve your reading comprehension and critical thinking skills. Also, because these exercises include items of the types often found on state and national tests, learning how to complete them will prepare you for tests you may have to take in the future.

How to Use This Book

About the Book.   *Deceptions* contains three units, each of which includes seven lessons. Each lesson begins with an article about an unusual event, person, or group. The article is followed by a group of four reading comprehension exercises and a set of three critical thinking exercises. The reading comprehension exercises will help you understand the article. The critical thinking exercises will help you think about what you have read and how it relates to your own experience.

At the end of the lesson, you will also have the opportunity to give your personal response to some aspect of the article and then to assess how well you understood what you read.

The Sample Lesson.   Working through the sample lesson, the first lesson in the book, with your class or group will demonstrate how a lesson is organized. The sample lesson explains how to complete the exercises and score your answers. The correct answers for the sample exercises and sample scores are printed in lighter type. In some cases, explanations of the correct answers are given. The explanations will help you understand how to think through these question types.

If you have any questions about how to complete the exercises or score them, this is the time to get the answers.

Working Through Each Lesson.   Begin each lesson by looking at the photographs and reading the captions. Before you read, predict what you think the article will be about. Then read the article.

Sometimes your teacher may decide to time your reading. Timing helps you keep track of and increase your reading speed. If you have been timed, enter your reading time in the box at the end of the lesson. Then use the Words-per-Minute Table to find your reading speed, and record your speed on the Reading Speed graph at the end of the unit.

Next complete the Reading Comprehension and Critical Thinking exercises. The directions for each exercise will tell you how to mark your answers. When you have finished all four Reading Comprehension exercises, use the answer key provided by your teacher to check your work. Follow the directions after each exercise to find your score. Record your Reading Comprehension scores on the graph at the end of each unit. Then check your answers to the Author's Approach, Summarizing and Paraphrasing, and Critical Thinking exercises. Fill in the Critical Thinking chart at the end of each unit with your evaluation of your work and comments about your progress.

At the end of each unit you will also complete a Compare/Contrast chart. The completed chart will help you see what the articles have in common. It will also give you an opportunity to explore your own ideas about deceivers and their deceptions.

SAMPLE LESSON

MILLI VANILLI

Milli Vanilli swept onto the music scene like a tornado. Few pop groups had risen so far, so fast. The duo's debut album, *Girl, You Know It's True,* sold seven million copies in the United States alone. It sold another three million worldwide. These sales earned Milli Vanilli a quick $2 million. In 1989, the group won a Grammy for Best New Artist.

2   The stars of Milli Vanilli were Fabrice "Fab" Morvan and Robert "Rob" Pilatus. The two men first met in 1986 at a nightclub in Los Angeles. Fab was an aspiring dancer from France. Rob was a musician from Germany. They became friends and decided to team up.

3   Their early efforts as a singing duo failed. But they struck gold with their first album, *Girl You Know It's True.* Suddenly, they had millions of fans around the world. There was only one problem: the album was a total fraud. Neither Fab nor Rob sang a single note of it. All they did was dance and lip-sync for the videos and "live" concerts.

Milli Vanilli singers Rob Pilatus (l) and Fabrice Morvan hold the Grammy Award they won as best new artists. They later returned the Grammy when it was discovered that they were not the actual singers on their recording.

4   According to Fab and Rob, the deception began with Frank Farian. He was the producer of the album. The duo said he enticed them to go along with the charade by promising them a chance to sing on their own later. "We were in the projects and had no money," said Rob. "[We made] a pact with the devil."

5   Farian, on the other hand, claimed that the idea for a fake album came from Fab and Rob. He said that they approached him, offering themselves as song-and-dance stand-ins. "They told me if I had good music to perform," said Farian, "they were there."

6   In the end, it didn't matter who had the idea first. They all agreed to go along with the ruse. And a clever ruse it was. Fab and Rob had much of what it took to be music stars. They were young—both 24 years old. They had just the right look. They dressed in hip European clothes and wore their hair in long stylish braids. They could also dance beautifully. The only thing they couldn't do was sing.

7   That was where Brad Howell and John Davis fit into the picture. At age 46 and 36, respectively, Howell and Davis were a little too old to appeal to rock's young fans. They were also a bit too pudgy. They wouldn't look good on the video. But their voices were fantastic. Knowing they could never be stars on their own, they agreed to be behind-the-scenes voices for Milli Vanilli. As Howell said, "Why not let the young boys please the young people?"

8   So Davis and Howell sang their parts. Meanwhile, in a separate studio, Fab and Rob mouthed the words and danced their hearts out in front of the video cameras. It was all done under tight security. Davis and Howell slipped out of the studio under the cover of darkness. Fab and Rob met Howell once. They never met Davis at all.

9   The deception worked—for a while. For almost two years Fab and Rob lived as the real Milli Vanilli. They appeared on TV to accept their Grammy. They signed autographs. They agreed to go on a 108-city tour across the United States. They also made plans to start work on their second album.

The "real" Milli Vanilli, John Davis (far left) and Brad Howell (far right)

10 But trouble was brewing for the two stars. Part of the problem was that Fab and Rob began to take themselves too seriously. They grew increasingly arrogant. At the Grammy awards, they thanked no one for their success. That upset the real singers, who could only watch on TV. John Davis felt that Fab and Rob should have at least said "thank you." Brad Howell agreed. "They didn't have to mention names," he said, "just the people behind the scenes."

11 By the end of 1990, the fraud finally came unglued. Too many people already knew, or suspected, that Milli Vanilli was a fake. Rumors began to circulate. TV talk show host Arsenio Hall openly made fun of the group. Some people wondered how a Frenchman and a German could sing so clearly in English.

12 Farian could see that Fab and Rob would never be able to pull off their U.S. tour. Their lip-syncing act couldn't last that long. Worse, they might actually try to sing themselves. That would be a dead giveaway. So Farian asked them not to do the tour. When Fab and Rob refused to cancel it, he fired them.

13 Now Frank Farian had no choice but to confess. The Great Milli Vanilli Caper was over. The Academy of Recording Arts and Sciences withdrew the Grammy. "I'm relieved that the truth has come out," said Farian. "It was a crazy idea, and I'm not going to do it again."

14 Farian said the scheme had failed because "the success was too big." In his words, "The situation became monstrous." He revealed that Fab and Rob wanted to sing for themselves on the second album. "Their voices aren't that good," said Farian. "I couldn't fulfill that condition."

15 Meanwhile, Milli Vanilli fans were outraged. Some returned albums and CDs, demanding their money back. One fan even filed a lawsuit alleging fraud. There was little that Fab and Rob could do, except to apologize. "We're really, really sorry about our fans," they pleaded publicly. "We love our fans. We just hope that they understand we were young and we wanted to live life the American way."

If you have been timed while reading this article, enter your reading time below. Then turn to the Words-per-Minute Table on page 71 and look up your reading speed (words per minute). Enter your reading speed on the graph on page 72.

Reading Time: Sample Lesson

_____ : _____
Minutes   Seconds

A Finding the Main Idea

One statement below expresses the main idea of the article. One statement is too general, or too broad. The other statement explains only part of the article; it is too narrow. Label the statements using the following key:

M—Main Idea   **B—Too Broad**   **N—Too Narrow**

_____N_____ 1. The duo called Milli Vanilli received the Grammy for Best New Artist in 1989 and didn't bother to thank the singers who really sang on their records. [This statement is *too narrow*. It focuses on only one incident from the article.]

_____B_____ 2. Modern technology makes it ever more possible to fool the buying public, as pop-rock group Milli Vanilli proved. [This statement is *too broad*. While true, the statement doesn't explain the nature of Milli Vanilli's deception.]

_____M_____ 3. Even though rock stars Milli Vanilli couldn't sing, they were able to fool music fans all over the world before their fraud was finally uncovered. [This statement is the *main idea*. It tells who Milli Vanilli were and what they did.]

_____15_____ Score 15 points for a correct M answer.

_____10_____ Score 5 points for each correct B or N answer.

_____25_____ **Total Score:** Finding the Main Idea

B Recalling Facts

How well do you remember the facts in the article? Put an X in the box next to the answer that correctly completes each statement about the article.

1. According to Fab and Rob, the first person to suggest the deception was
   - ☐ a. Fab himself.
   - ☒ b. the album producer, Frank Farian.
   - ☐ c. Brad Howell, the real singer.

2. Brad Howell and John Davis felt they could not be rock stars because they
   - ☐ a. were terrible dancers.
   - ☒ b. were too old and didn't look the part.
   - ☐ c. did not enjoy the excitement of touring with a band.

3. The real singers were upset when Milli Vanilli received the Grammy because
   - ☒ a. Fab and Rob didn't thank anyone else for their success.
   - ☐ b. they were afraid that the deception would be uncovered.
   - ☐ c. they wanted credit for the singing themselves.

4. Frank Farian finally was forced to confess that Milli Vanilli was a fraud when
   - ☐ a. The Academy of Recording Arts and Sciences threatened to investigate the group.
   - ☐ b. On stage, Fab and Rob forgot the words to a song.
   - ☒ c. Fab and Rob insisted on singing on tour.

5. When Milli Vanilli fans found out they had been fooled, they
   - ☒ a. became upset and angry.
   - ☐ b. quickly forgave Fab and Rob.
   - ☐ c. continued to buy Milli Vanilli records.

Score 5 points for each correct answer.

_____25_____ **Total Score:** Recalling Facts

C | Making Inferences

When you combine your own experience and information from a text to draw a conclusion that is not directly stated in that text, you are making an inference. Below are five statements that may or may not be inferences based on information in the article. Label the statements using the following key:

C—Correct Inference   **F—Faulty Inference**

_F_ 1. Fab and Rob would have done anything, no matter how illegal or deceitful, to become rock stars. [This is a *faulty* inference. You cannot tell for sure what they were willing to do for fame.]

_F_ 2. Frank Farian has probably tried to fool the public with other singers in the years since the Milli Vanilli caper. [This is a *faulty* inference. Just because he fooled the public once doesn't mean he fooled it again. He may have learned his lesson.]

_C_ 3. A singer's voice can still appeal to young audiences even when the singer is no longer young. [This is a *correct* inference. The young audiences enjoyed the voices of the real Milli Vanilli singers who were 46 and 36 years old—no longer young by the usual standards of rock.]

_F_ 4. If Fab and Rob had agreed to continue lip-syncing, they definitely would still be big stars. [This is a *faulty* inference. Too many factors contribute to success to be sure about the group's future popularity.]

_C_ 5. It is possible that other acts have used lip-syncing while the real singers are never seen. [This is a *correct* inference. Other singers who tricked the public this way may not have been exposed.]

Score 5 points for each correct answer.

_25_ **Total Score:** Making Inferences

D | Using Words Precisely

Each numbered sentence below contains an underlined word or phrase from the article. Following the sentence are three definitions. One definition is closest to the meaning of the underlined word. One definition is opposite or nearly opposite. Label those two definitions using the following key. Do not label the remaining definition.

C—Closest   **O—Opposite or Nearly Opposite**

1. The duo's <u>debut</u> album, *Girl, You Know It's True*, sold 7 million copies in the United States alone.

_O_ a. last

_C_ b. first

___ c. successful

2. The duo said he <u>enticed</u> them to go along with the charade by promising them a chance to sing on their own later.

_O_ a. advised against

___ b. frightened

_C_ c. persuaded

3. They all agreed to go along with the <u>ruse</u>.

_C_ a. trick

___ b. game

_O_ c. honest activity

4. They grew increasingly <u>arrogant</u>.

_C_ a. conceited

_O_ b. humble

___ c. nervous

5. One fan even filed a lawsuit <u>alleging</u> fraud.

_____ a. proving

___0___ b. denying

___C___ c. claiming

___15___ Score 3 points for each correct C answer.

___10___ Score 2 points for each correct O answer.

___25___ **Total Score:** Using Words Precisely

Enter the four total scores in the spaces below, and add them together to find your Reading Comprehension Score. Then record your score on the graph on page 73.

Score	Question Type	Sample Lesson
25	Finding the Main Idea	
25	Recalling Facts	
25	Making Inferences	
25	Using Words Precisely	
100	**Reading Comprehension Score**	

Author's Approach

Put an X in the box next to the correct answer.

1. What does the author mean by the statement "Milli Vanilli swept onto the music scene like a tornado"?

☐ a. Milli Vanilli caused a great deal of damage.

☒ b. Milli Vanilli became popular very quickly.

☐ c. Milli Vanilli destroyed all their competition in the music business.

2. What is the author's purpose in writing "Milli Vanilli"?

☐ a. To encourage the reader to doubt the truthfulness of any performer

☒ b. To inform the reader about one deception in the music business

☐ c. To describe a situation in which innocent dancers were deceived by a ruthless producer

3. From the statements below, choose the one that you believe the author would agree with.

☐ a. The Academy of Recording Arts and Sciences always investigates artists thoroughly before giving awards.

☒ b. Pride goes before a fall.

☐ c. The public doesn't care if celebrities tell them the truth or not.

4. In this article, "the people behind the scenes" means

☒ a. people who worked hard but got no recognition.

☐ b. people who refused to believe that Milli Vanilli were really singing their own songs.

☐ c. people who gave Milli Vanilli the Grammy award.

___4___ Number of correct answers

Record your personal assessment of your work on the Critical Thinking Chart on page 74.

Summarizing and Paraphrasing

Follow the directions provided for question 1. Put an X in the box next to the correct answer for the other question.

1. Complete the following one-sentence summary of the article using the lettered phrases from the phrase bank below. Write the letters on the lines.

> **Phrase Bank:**
> a. how Fab and Rob reacted to their success
> b. the downfall of Milli Vanilli
> c. a description of Milli Vanilli's successes and their early years

The article about Milli Vanilli begins with _____c_____, goes on to explain _____a_____, and ends with _____b_____.

2. Choose the sentence that correctly restates the following sentence from the article:

"That would be a dead giveaway."

☒ a. That action would be sure to reveal the secret.

☐ b. That action would cause the death of one of the performers.

☐ c. That action would cause a great deal of sorrow.

> _____4_____ Number of correct answers
>
> Record your personal assessment of your work on the Critical Thinking Chart on page 74.

Critical Thinking

Put an X in the box next to the correct answers for questions 1, 2, and 5. Follow the directions provided for the other questions.

1. Which of the following statements from the article is an opinion rather than a fact?

☐ a. Fab and Rob met Howell once.

☒ b. They had just the right look. [This statement is an opinion—it cannot be proved.]

☐ c. For almost two years Fab and Rob lived as the real Milli Vanilli.

2. From what Frank Farian said after the fraud was revealed, you can predict that he will

☐ a. give up show business forever.

☐ b. work harder to cover up future ruses.

☒ c. not ask dancers to stand in for singers in the future.

3. Choose from the letters below to correctly complete the following statement. Write the letters on the lines.

On the positive side, _____c_____, but on the negative side _____a_____.

a. Milli Vanilli were not honest with the public

b. Frank Farian produced Milli Vanilli's first album

c. Milli Vanilli created some enjoyable music

4. Read paragraph 12. Then choose from the letters below to correctly complete the following statement. Write the letters on the lines.

According to paragraph 12, _____c_____ because _____b_____.

a. Milli Vanilli were planning a U.S. tour

b. Fab and Rob refused to agree not to sing themselves

c. Frank Farian fired Fab and Rob

5. What did you have to do to answer question 1?

☒ a. find an opinion (what someone thinks about something)

☐ b. find a description (how something looks)

☐ c. draw a conclusion (a sensible statement based on the text and your experience)

_____7_____ Number of correct answers

Record your personal assessment of your work on the Critical Thinking Chart on page 74.

Record your personal assessment of your work on the Critical Thinking Chart on page 74.

Self-Assessment

From reading this article, I have learned

[Record any idea or fact that you learned from the article.]

_____

_____

_____

Personal Response

I can't believe

[Record any detail that you found difficult to believe.]

_____

_____

_____

Self-Assessment

To get the most out of the Critical Reading series program, you need to take charge of your own progress in improving your reading comprehension and critical thinking skills. Here are some of the features that help you work on those essential skills.

Reading Comprehension Exercises. Complete these exercises immediately after reading the article. They help you recall what you have read, understand the stated and implied main ideas, and add words to your working vocabulary.

Critical Thinking Skills Exercises. These exercises help you focus on the author's approach and purpose, recognize and generate summaries and paraphrases, and identify relationships between ideas.

Personal Response and Self-assessment. Questions in this category help you relate the articles to your personal experience and give you the opportunity to evaluate your understanding of the information in that lesson.

Compare and Contrast Charts. At the end of each unit you will complete a Compare and Contrast chart. The completed chart helps you see what the articles have in common and gives you an opportunity to explore your own ideas about the topics discussed in the articles.

The Graphs. The graphs and charts at the end of each unit enable you to keep track of your progress. Check your graphs regularly with your teacher. Decide whether your progress is satisfactory or whether you need additional work on some skills. What types of exercises are you having difficulty with? Talk with your teacher about ways to work on the skills in which you need the most practice.

UNIT ONE

P.T. BARNUM
The Prince of Humbug

Phineas Taylor Barnum had a unique approach to life. He looked at it this way: if he told a little white lie, no one would believe him, but if he told a real whopper, people would fall for it. P. T. Barnum spent most of his life telling one big whopper after another. It made him both rich and famous. "My dear sir," he once said, "the bigger the humbug, the better the people will like it." If nothing else, P. T. Barnum was the true "Prince of Humbug."

2   Barnum pulled off his first hoax in 1835. It began when he found an old, blind, and badly-crippled African-American woman. Her name was Joice Heth. Barnum devised a clever scheme to make a lot of money using this elderly lady.

3   He put an ad in all the New York City newspapers. The ad promised "the most astonishing and interesting curiosity in the World!" It was this: Barnum had found George Washington's nurse. The ad claimed that Joice Heth had been born in 1674. That made her 161 years old. Barnum further claimed that this woman of "unparalleled longevity" was the first person "who put clothes on [little George]." Although she now weighed "but

forty-six pounds," she was "very cheerful." And, better yet, for a small price, the reader could see her at the Masonic Hall.

4   Was Joice Heth really George Washington's nurse? Of course, Barnum insisted. He had the "authentic and indisputable documents" to prove it.

5   Thousands of people rushed to catch a glimpse of this historic woman. For a while, Barnum made a handsome profit. In time, though, interest in Joice Heth began to fade. Admission sales went down. Then an anonymous letter appeared in all the papers. It claimed that Joice Seth was a complete fraud. In fact, the letter said, Joice Seth wasn't a real person at all. She was just "[an] automaton, made up of whalebone, India rubber, and numberless springs." Her voice was the trick of "a ventriloquist." As a result of this letter, people flocked back to get a second look. Few knew that the author of the anonymous letter was P. T. Barnum himself.

6   Joice Seth was not made of whalebone and rubber, of course. But neither was she George Washington's nurse. All the documents that "proved" her identity were fakes. Also, when Joice Seth died a year later, a famous surgeon examined her body. He declared that she was "probably not over 80." But Barnum didn't care. He

had entertained people and had made a great deal of money. Besides, he had already moved on to other things.

P. T. Barnum, creator of the Greatest Show on Earth, with Commodore Nutt, a performer in Barnum's show, in 1862

A circus poster advertising the Barnum & Bailey Greatest Show on Earth

7   Barnum spent much of his life looking for the truly bizarre and grotesque. Finding them was the easy part. The hard part was promoting these oddities into "the world's greatest" this or that. This was where Barnum showed his true genius. He rose head and shoulders above the other showmen of his time. Some people even called him "The Shakespeare of Advertising."

8   One of P. T. Barnum's great inventions was Tom Thumb. In 1842, he found a five-year-old boy named Charles Stratton who weighed 15 pounds and stood less than two feet tall. Barnum made a deal with the boy's parents to put the child on tour. Soon the little boy had become "General Tom Thumb, a dwarf of 11 years, just arrived from England." Stratton was a midget, not a dwarf, but such minor details never bothered P. T. Barnum.

9   Before long, Barnum had turned Tom Thumb into a major attraction. In 1844, Barnum took him to England. There he put him on display at London's Egyptian Hall. Benjamin Haydon, a famous artist, was there, too. Haydon had his own art exhibit for people to see. But no one bothered with Haydon's work. People "rush by thousands to see Tom Thumb," wrote Haydon in his journal. "They push, they fight, they scream, they cry help and murder! and oh! and ah!" Later, a depressed Haydon took out a pistol and shot himself in the head. Barnum, of course, used the suicide scandal to further promote Tom Thumb.

10   Nothing was ever too tasteless for Barnum. He would exploit anyone or anything. He wanted to show "all that is monstrous, scaly, strange, and queer." He especially loved what he called "freaks." For instance, he showcased Jo-Jo the Dog-Faced Boy. He showcased Chang and Eng, the first Siamese twins known to survive to adulthood. And he showcased the Wild Men of Borneo. These two pathetic men had never been near Borneo. They were just two retarded brothers from Ohio.

11   If the real world wasn't odd enough, Barnum created his own oddities. One famous example was the Feejee Mermaid. It was simply a monkey's head sewn to a fish's body. Barnum enticed customers into the exhibit with an 18-foot poster. Once inside, all they could see was a dried-up 18-inch specimen. Still, people stood in long lines to see it.

12   P. T. Barnum had more than one way to fool his customers. He got away with it because he was smarter than most of them. His whole career was based on a simple principle: "There's a sucker born every minute." He was right. People paid money to see "the horse with its head where its tail ought to be." What they saw was a normal horse with its tail in a feeding stall.

13   P. T. Barnum also had a sense of humor. He loved to put up a sign that read: "This Way to the Egress." He would put it next to signs that read: "This Way to the Lioness" or "This Way to the Tigress." Lots of curious people had never seen an "egress." So they followed the sign through a door, only to find themselves back out on the street. It cost them another 25 cents to reenter the hall. But at least they now knew that the word "egress" is just a fancy word for "exit."

If you have been timed while reading this article, enter your reading time below. Then turn to the Words-per-Minute Table on page 71 and look up your reading speed (words per minute). Enter your reading speed on the graph on page 72.

Reading Time: Lesson 1

_____ : _____
Minutes   Seconds

A Finding the Main Idea

One statement below expresses the main idea of the article. One statement is too general, or too broad. The other statement explains only part of the article; it is too narrow. Label the statements using the following key:

M—Main Idea   **B—Too Broad**   **N—Too Narrow**

_____ 1. P. T. Barnum was a master showman who could fool people and still entertain them.

_____ 2. P. T. Barnum promoted oddities such as the Feejee Mermaid into popular sideshow acts.

_____ 3. The life of P. T. Barnum proves that, at times, people don't mind being fooled.

_____ Score 15 points for a correct M answer.

_____ Score 5 points for each correct B or N answer.

_____ **Total Score:** Finding the Main Idea

B Recalling Facts

How well do you remember the facts in the article? Put an X in the box next to the answer that correctly completes each statement about the article.

1. P. T. Barnum claimed that Joice Heth was
    - ☐ a. George Washington's mother.
    - ☐ b. George Washington's nurse.
    - ☐ c. George Washington's daughter.

2. When Barnum found a five-year-old midget, he advertised him as
    - ☐ a. the Wild Man of Borneo.
    - ☐ b. an automaton.
    - ☐ c. General Tom Thumb.

3. When the crowds coming to see Joice Heth decreased, Barnum
    - ☐ a. found another performer to take her place.
    - ☐ b. wrote a letter to the papers claiming she was a rubber dummy.
    - ☐ c. advertised her as a ventriloquist.

4. Barnum took General Tom Thumb on tour to
    - ☐ a. India.
    - ☐ b. Egypt.
    - ☐ c. England.

5. After people at Barnum's shows followed the signs to the egress, they
    - ☐ a. were directed to the lioness and the tigress.
    - ☐ b. were treated to the sight of a female egret.
    - ☐ c. had to buy another ticket to get back into the show.

Score 5 points for each correct answer.

_____ **Total Score:** Recalling Facts

C Making Inferences

When you combine your own experience and information from a text to draw a conclusion that is not directly stated in that text, you are making an inference. Below are five statements that may or may not be inferences based on information in the article. Label the statements using the following key:

C—Correct Inference   F—Faulty Inference

_____ 1. Only Americans enjoyed seeing the oddities that P. T. Barnum put on display.

_____ 2. P. T. Barnum was always mindful of the feelings of his performers.

_____ 3. You can't always believe what you read in the newspapers.

_____ 4. When people find out that they have been fooled, they are always angry.

_____ 5. P. T. Barnum believed that it was morally acceptable to tell lies.

Score 5 points for each correct answer.

_____ **Total Score:** Making Inferences

D Using Words Precisely

Each numbered sentence below contains an underlined word or phrase from the article. Following the sentence are three definitions. One definition is closest to the meaning of the underlined word. One definition is opposite or nearly opposite. Label those two definitions using the following key. Do not label the remaining definition.

C—Closest   O—Opposite or Nearly Opposite

1. Then an <u>anonymous</u> letter appeared in all the papers.

_____ a. signed

_____ b. written by an unknown person

_____ c. angry

2. Barnum spent much of his life looking for the truly <u>bizarre</u> and grotesque.

_____ a. common

_____ b. expensive

_____ c. unusual

3. He would <u>exploit</u> anyone or anything.

_____ a. take advantage of

_____ b. get excited about

_____ c. come to the aid of

4. He <u>showcased</u> Change and Eng, the first Siamese twins known to survive to adulthood.

_____ a. featured in a special show

_____ b. drew attention away from

_____ c. discovered

5. These two <u>pathetic</u> men had never been near Borneo.

_____ a. local

_____ b. pitiful

_____ c. strong and confident

_____ Score 3 points for each correct C answer.

_____ Score 2 points for each correct O answer.

_____ **Total Score:** Using Words Precisely

Enter the four total scores in the spaces below, and add them together to find your Reading Comprehension Score. Then record your score on the graph on page 73.

Score	Question Type	Lesson 1
_____	Finding the Main Idea	
_____	Recalling Facts	
_____	Making Inferences	
_____	Using Words Precisely	
_____	**Reading Comprehension Score**	

Author's Approach

Put an X in the box next to the correct answer.

1. The main purpose of the first paragraph is to
   - ☐ a. inform readers about P. T. Barnum's habit of telling lies for profit.
   - ☐ b. explain how P. T. Barnum fooled the public with his strange performers.
   - ☐ c. make readers dislike P. T. Barnum.

2. Judging from statements in the article "P. T. Barnum: The Prince of Humbug," you can conclude that the author wants the reader to think that
   - ☐ a. any activity is all right as long as it makes a profit.
   - ☐ b. people in the nineteenth century were not as smart as people today.
   - ☐ c. P. T. Barnum was a clever and inventive entertainer.

3. The author tells this story mainly by
   - ☐ a. retelling personal experiences.
   - ☐ b. comparing different topics.
   - ☐ c. telling different stories about the same topic.

_____ Number of correct answers

Record your personal assessment of your work on the Critical Thinking Chart on page 74.

Summarizing and Paraphrasing

Follow the directions provided for question 1. Put an X in the box next to the correct answer for the other questions.

1. Look for the important ideas and events in paragraphs 5 and 6. Summarize those paragraphs in one or two sentences.

_____

_____

_____

2. Below are summaries of the article. Choose the summary that says all the most important things about the article but in the fewest words.

☐ a. P. T. Barnum was often called the Prince of Humbug because he didn't care about telling the truth.

☐ b. P. T. Barnum, known as "The Prince of Humbug," was able to convince people all over the world to believe in his unusual and misleading shows. Some of the acts he featured in his shows were General Tom Thumb, the Feejee Mermaid, and the horse with its head where its tail ought to be.

☐ c. P. T. Barnum, a showman in 1800s, discovered oddities and displayed them for an admission fee. He was an expert at fooling the public in an entertaining way.

3. Read the statement about the article below. Then read the paraphrase of that statement. Choose the reason that best tells why the paraphrase does not say the same thing as the statement.

Statement: P. T. Barnum was a genius when it came to creative advertising.

Paraphrase: P. T. Barnum was an extremely talented man.

☐ a. Paraphrase says too much.

☐ b. Paraphrase doesn't say enough.

☐ c. Paraphrase doesn't agree with the statement about the article.

_____
_____ Number of correct answers

Record your personal assessment of your work on the Critical Thinking Chart on page 74.

Critical Thinking

Follow the directions provided for questions 1 and 5. Put an X in the box next to the correct answer for the other questions.

1. For each statement below, write O if it expresses an opinion and write F if it expresses a fact.

_____ a. Nothing was ever too tasteless for Barnum.

_____ b. Barnum had more than one way to fool his customers.

_____ c. Barnum enticed customers into the exhibit with an 18-foot poster.

2. From the article, you can predict that if P. T. Barnum had claimed that he had men from Mars in his show

☐ a. no one would have believed him because the claim was too ridiculous.

☐ b. some people would have believed him and paid to see them.

☐ c. those creatures really would have existed.

3. What might have been the cause of Benjamin Haydon's suicide?

☐ a. He became depressed because people ignored his work on their way to see Tom Thumb.

☐ b. He wanted to go on tour with Barnum but was passed over.

☐ c. He was afraid of the people rushing to see Tom Thumb.

4. Of the following theme categories, which would this story fit into?

☐ a. adventure

☐ b. courage

☐ c. trickery

5. In which paragraph did you find your information or details to answer question 3?

_____

_____ Number of correct answers

Record your personal assessment of your work on the Critical Thinking Chart on page 74.

Personal Response

If you could ask the author of the article one question, what would it be?

_____

_____

_____

_____

Self-Assessment

I can't really understand how

_____

_____

_____

_____

SARAH EMMA EDMONDS
Union Spy

Franklin "Frank" Thompson loved his new country, the United States. At the age of 19, he had run away from his family farm in Canada to escape a cruel father. Thompson settled in Flint, Michigan, where he sold Bibles to earn a living. Then, in April 1861, the Civil War broke out between the North and the South. Frank Thompson wanted to help the Union. So he joined the 2nd Michigan Infantry as a field nurse and mail carrier.

2   Thompson's unit saw action right away. It took part in the First Battle of Bull Run. Later, it fought in the Peninsula campaign as well as at Fair Oaks and Fredericksburg. Still, Thompson's role was limited. He wanted to be more active in the war. So when a Union spy was shot in Virginia, Thompson agreed to take his place behind enemy lines.

3   For his first mission, Thompson dyed his head, neck, hands, and arms black. He put on a black wig and some old, threadbare clothes. Then he slipped behind enemy lines disguised as a slave named Ned. His job was to spy on Southern troop movements in and around Yorktown, Virginia. The North wanted to capture the Southern city of Richmond.

Sarah Emma Edmonds as herself (left) and disguised as Frank Thompson

But the forces at Yorktown blocked the way. So it was vital to know what these troops might do.

4   Thompson made notes and sketches of the things he saw and hid his writings in his boot. But his disguise soon backfired. Southern troops put this "slave" in a work gang. Worse, his dye quickly began to fade. If Thompson's true identity were discovered, he would be shot just like any other spy. Luckily, he was left alone on the third night. Under the cover of darkness, he managed to slip back over to the Northern side of the line.

5   Frank Thompson swore he would never go back to the South as a male. It was far too risky. Young males who were not soldiers were too conspicuous. So when he went back a second time to spy, Thompson posed as an Irish peddler woman named Bridget who sold cakes and pies. This new disguise was more convenient in two ways. First, Thompson didn't have to worry about his black dye fading. And second, going as a woman came naturally. That was because Frank Thompson *was* a woman.

6   Thompson's real name was Sarah Emma Edmonds. Edmonds had begun disguising herself as a man soon after she ran away from the family farm. She sold Bibles as a man. And she joined the army as a man. For a long time, no one in the

army knew Thompson's real identity. Gradually, a few close friends discovered the truth. Jerome Robbins, an army

Sarah Emma Edmonds disguised as an African American worker in the Confederate lines.

comrade, wrote in his diary "my friend Frank is a female." Still, most people didn't learn of the deception until many years after the war.

7   On her second spy mission, "Bridget" came across a Southern soldier who was dying of fever in an abandoned house. She nursed the man during his final hours. The soldier made one last request. Would "Bridget" return his gold watch to his commanding officer? She agreed. When Southern officers came to retrieve the body, "Bridget" guided them to the house. They asked her to stay outside to be on the lookout for Union troops. As soon as the men had gone inside, "Bridget" hopped onto one of their horses and dashed to the Union side with fresh news of enemy plans.

8   On another spy mission, Edmonds disguised herself as an African-American woman. She got a job as a cook serving Southern officers. As they ate their meals and discussed their plans, Edmonds took mental notes. As soon as she had enough information, she disappeared back to the Union side. In all, she went on about a dozen spy missions, each time using a new disguise.

9   In 1863, Edmonds fell sick with malaria. She feared that a trip to the doctor would reveal that she was a woman. So Edmonds asked for a leave of absence from the army. The request was turned down. Edmonds then faced a difficult decision. She could see an army doctor and have the truth exposed. Or she could desert the army and go to a civilian doctor. The truth, she feared, might lead to a dishonorable discharge. So, on April 22, 1863, she deserted.

10   In time, Edmonds recovered from malaria. She resumed her life as a nurse and a woman. She found work in a hospital. There she cared for wounded soldiers. Before the war ended, she also wrote a highly colorful book about her life. It was called *Nurse and Spy in the Union Army*. The book sold more than 175,000 copies. After the war, Edmonds married Linus Seelye. They had three children, but all died young.

11   Despite the book, it was not until 1882 that the story of Frank Thompson became widely known. At that time, Edmonds was living in Kansas. She wanted to apply for a pension for her service in the Civil War. So she wrote to some of her old army friends. They came to her defense and even invited her to a reunion party. Many also wrote to the army and to Congress. They testified to her good moral character.

A few noted that they had never realized her true sex.

12   Soon the army dropped the charges of desertion against her. In 1884, Congress ordered that the name "Sarah E. E. Seelye, alias Franklin Thompson" be placed on the pension role. For the rest of her life, the government paid her $12 a month. Sarah Edmonds had lived a lie. But she had done it for a noble purpose—to serve her adopted country. Her book made her the most famous woman to fight in the Civil War. But she wasn't the only one. One estimate suggests that as many as 400 other women did the same thing. 🍃

If you have been timed while reading this article, enter your reading time below. Then turn to the Words-per-Minute Table on page 71 and look up your reading speed (words per minute). Enter your reading speed on the graph on page 72.

Reading Time: Lesson 2

_____ : _____
Minutes   Seconds

A | Finding the Main Idea

One statement below expresses the main idea of the article. One statement is too general, or too broad. The other statement explains only part of the article; it is too narrow. Label the statements using the following key:

M—Main Idea   **B—Too Broad**   **N—Too Narrow**

_____ 1. Sarah Emma Edmonds was a courageous citizen who served her adopted country well during time of war.

_____ 2. Sarah Emma Edmonds first disguised herself as a man when she ran away from the family farm in Canada.

_____ 3. Sarah Emma Edmonds, sometimes disguised as a man and sometimes as a woman, served the Union forces as a spy during the Civil War.

_____ Score 15 points for a correct M answer.

_____ Score 5 points for each correct B or N answer.

_____ **Total Score:** Finding the Main Idea

B | Recalling Facts

How well do you remember the facts in the article? Put an X in the box next to the answer that correctly completes each statement about the article.

1. On Frank Thompson's first spy mission, he dressed as
   - ☐ a. an African-American cook.
   - ☐ b. a slave.
   - ☐ c. an Irish peddler named Bridget.

2. The number of spy missions that Sarah Emma Edmonds completed was about
   - ☐ a. 12.
   - ☐ b. 4.
   - ☐ c. 30.

3. When Sarah Emma Edmonds came down with malaria, she
   - ☐ a. deserted the army immediately.
   - ☐ b. visited a doctor who discovered she was really a woman.
   - ☐ c. asked the army for a leave of absence.

4. After leaving the army, Sarah did all of the following except
   - ☐ a. fight for the South.
   - ☐ b. write a book about her experiences.
   - ☐ c. marry and have children.

5. In 1884, Sarah Edmonds was pleased that the army
   - ☐ a. announced that she was the only woman who had served the Union army as a spy.
   - ☐ b. gave her a medal for bravery.
   - ☐ c. awarded her a pension.

Score 5 points for each correct answer.

_____ **Total Score:** Recalling Facts

C | Making Inferences

When you combine your own experience and information from a text to draw a conclusion that is not directly stated in that text, you are making an inference. Below are five statements that may or may not be inferences based on information in the article. Label the statements using the following key:

C—Correct Inference   F—Faulty Inference

_____ 1. Women make better spies than men do.

_____ 2. Edmonds was probably a very small woman.

_____ 3. Edmonds was more adventurous than most people.

_____ 4. Soldiers in the Union army did not undergo thorough physical exams.

_____ 5. You could buy much more with a dollar in 1884 than you can today.

Score 5 points for each correct answer.

_____ **Total Score:** Making Inferences

D | Using Words Precisely

Each numbered sentence below contains an underlined word or phrase from the article. Following the sentence are three definitions. One definition is closest to the meaning of the underlined word. One definition is opposite or nearly opposite. Label those two definitions using the following key. Do not label the remaining definition.

C—Closest   O—Opposite or Nearly Opposite

1. He put on a black wig and some old, underline threadbare clothes.

_____ a. well-worn

_____ b. loose-fitting

_____ c. brand-new

2. Young males who were not soldiers were too conspicuous.

_____ a. obvious

_____ b. hard to spot

_____ c. cowardly

3. Jerome Robbins, an army comrade, wrote in his diary "my friend Frank is a female."

_____ a. enemy

_____ b. reporter

_____ c. fellow soldier

4. She could see an army doctor and have the truth exposed.

_____ a. revealed

_____ b. hidden

_____ c. made fun of

5. They <u>testified to</u> her good moral character.

_____ a. practiced

_____ b. stood up for

_____ c. denied

_____ Score 3 points for each correct C answer.

_____ Score 2 points for each correct O answer.

_____ **Total Score:** Using Words Precisely

Enter the four total scores in the spaces below, and add them together to find your Reading Comprehension Score. Then record your score on the graph on page 73.

Score	Question Type	Lesson 2
_____	Finding the Main Idea	
_____	Recalling Facts	
_____	Making Inferences	
_____	Using Words Precisely	
_____	**Reading Comprehension Score**	

Author's Approach

Put an X in the box next to the correct answer.

1. The author uses the first sentence of the article to

☐ a. inform the reader that Frank Thompson was born in another country.

☐ b. describe the qualities of Frank Thompson.

☐ c. entertain the reader with interesting stories about Frank Thompson.

2. What does the author mean by the statement "As they ate their meals and discussed their plans, Edmonds took mental notes"?

☐ a. As the officers talked, Edmonds wrote down what she learned about enemy plans.

☐ b. As the officers talked, Edmonds secretly stole their notes about battle plans.

☐ c. As the officers talked, Edmonds tried to remember everything she heard.

3. How is the author's purpose for writing the article expressed in paragraph 12?

☐ a. The paragraph explains that Edmonds received an army pension.

☐ b. The paragraph mentions that the army dropped the charges of desertion against Edmonds.

☐ c. The paragraph explains that Edmonds lived a lie, but for a noble purpose.

4. The author probably wrote this article in order to

☐ a. prove that many women would rather be men.

☐ b. tell the story of a fascinating person.

☐ c. reveal injustices in the army's pension program.

_____ Number of correct answers

Record your personal assessment of your work on the Critical Thinking Chart on page 74.

Summarizing and Paraphrasing

Follow the directions provided for questions 1 and 2. Put an X in the box next to the correct answer for question 3.

1. Look for the important ideas and events in paragraphs 7 and 8. Summarize those paragraphs in one or two sentences.

_____

_____

_____

2. Complete the following one-sentence summary of the article using the lettered phrases from the phrase bank below. Write the letters on the lines.

Phrase Bank:
a. how Edmonds served the Union as a spy
b. the reasons for Edmonds's desertion from the army
c. the Union army awarding Edmonds a pension

The article about Sarah Emma Edmonds begins with _____, goes on to explain _____, and ends with _____.

3. Choose the best one-sentence paraphrase for the following sentence from the article:

"Thompson's unit saw action right away."

☐ a. Thompson's unit took part in some battles immediately.

☐ b. Thompson's unit soon witnessed some battles.

☐ c. Thompson made sure that his unit took part in military action right away.

_____ Number of correct answers

Record your personal assessment of your work on the Critical Thinking Chart on page 74.

Critical Thinking

Follow the directions provided for questions 1 and 2. Put an X in the box next to the correct answer for the other questions.

1. Choose from the letters below to correctly complete the following statement. Write the letters on the lines.

On the positive side, _____, but on the negative side _____.

a. Edmonds found out important information about enemy plans

b. Edmonds was born in Canada

c. Edmonds lived a lie

2. Read paragraph 9. Then choose from the letters below to correctly complete the following statement. Write the letters on the lines.

According to paragraph 9, _____ happened because _____.

a. the army would not grant her a leave of absence

b. Edmonds went on several spy missions as a woman

c. Edmonds decided to desert

3. Of the following theme categories, which would this article fit into?

☐ a. adventure

☐ b. humor

☐ c. science

4. What did you have to do to answer question 2?

☐ a. find a description (how something looks)

☐ b. draw a conclusion (a sensible statement based on the text and your experience)

☐ c. find an effect (something that happened)

_____ Number of correct answers

Record your personal assessment of your work on the Critical Thinking Chart on page 74.

Personal Response

This article is different from other articles about the Civil War I've read because

_____

_____

_____

_____

and Sarah Emma Edmonds is unlike other 19th-century women because

_____

_____

_____

_____

Self-Assessment

I'm proud of how I answered question # _____ in section _____

because _____

_____

_____

_____

THE TROJAN HORSE

Helen of Troy and Priam from a detail on a Greek cup. Priam was the father of 50 sons, one of whom was Paris, Helen's abductor.

The Trojan War took place more than 3,000 years ago. Yet the events of that struggle still spice our language. Today the term "Trojan horse" means a deadly ploy or deception. The warning to "beware of Greeks bearing gifts" also comes from the Trojan War. It means to watch out if someone gives you something that appears too good to be true.

2 The story of the Trojan War is a legend. We don't know for sure that it took place. It was said to be a war between the Greeks and the Trojans, resulting in the destruction of the Trojans' city of Troy. In 1870, experts uncovered ruins from Troy. So we know Troy was a real place. It is also quite likely that the Greeks and the Trojans did fight a war. They would have been natural rivals for control of the Aegean Sea. Beyond that, however, everything we know about the Trojan War comes from epic Greek poems.

3 According to the poems, the Trojan War began as a love story. A Trojan prince named Paris fell in love with a beautiful Greek woman named Helen of Sparta. Sparta was a powerful city in Greece. This was a legendary time when gods mixed

freely with humans. The gods did favors for humans they liked and punished those they didn't. The goddess Aphrodite liked Paris, so she promised to help him win the love of Helen.

4   There was a problem, however. Helen already had a husband. She was married to Sparta's King Menelaus. Still, Aphrodite urged Paris to go after Helen. She helped him set sail for Sparta. When Paris arrived there, King Menelaus welcomed him. Soon, though, the king was called away. The king told his wife to entertain their guest. Instead, Helen fell in love with him. The two lovers then fled to Troy.

5   Menelaus was enraged when he heard what had happened. With the help of some goddess friends of his own, Menelaus rallied the Greeks to get his wife back. He pulled together 1,186 ships and more than a hundred thousand men. Thus it was said that Helen was so lovely that "her face launched a thousand ships."

6   Menelaus's group included several famous Greek heroes. There was Agamemnon, leader of the army. There was Achilles, the greatest of the Greek warriors. And there was the clever Odysseus.

7   The Trojans, meanwhile, had also lined up some brave men to fight on their side. The Trojans were led by Paris and the courageous Hector. Although the Greeks outnumbered the Trojans, they couldn't defeat them. The best the Greeks could do was put the city of Troy under siege. The siege dragged on for nine long years. Despite help from the gods, neither side could gain and keep the upper hand.

8   The situation changed in the tenth year. An argument broke out between Achilles and Agamemnon. Achilles refused to fight anymore. The Greeks began to lose heart. Achilles's friend Patroclus tried to rally them. He put on Achilles's armor, hoping to inspire the Greek troops to keep fighting. Instead, Patroclus died at the hands of Hector.

9   Ashamed and upset by the death of his dear friend, Achilles rejoined the battle. He killed Hector with a spear, then shouted, "So shall all dogs die!"

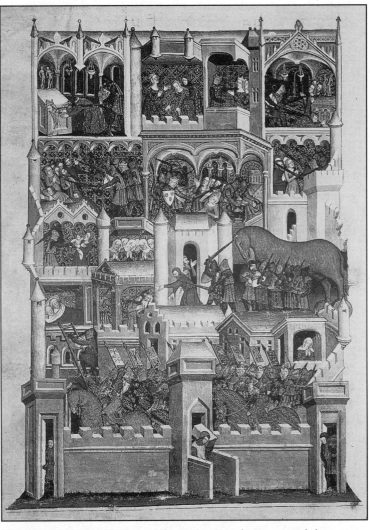

The story of Helen of Troy and the Trojan War has captured the imaginations of people throughout history. This scene was painted in the 14th century.

Hector's body was dragged around the walls of Troy three times. Everyone was shocked by such brutal treatment of a fallen foe.

10 The gods, too, were stunned by these latest events. The god Apollo leaped into the battle on the side of the Trojans. He guided a poison arrow fired by Paris. It struck Achilles in the heel, his only weak spot, killing him. Later, Paris was himself killed by an arrow. As the fighting raged back and forth, it seemed the war would never end. Then, suddenly, it did.

11 One morning when the Trojans looked over their walls, everything was calm. They were astonished to see that all the Greeks were gone. Nothing was left but an empty camp. Even the Greek ships were gone. Then the Trojans spotted the one thing that the Greeks had left behind. It was a gigantic wooden horse. The horse was mounted on a platform with wooden wheels. On the side of the horse there was a message to the goddess Athena. It was a prayer for the safe return of the Greek army to Greece.

12 At first, the Trojans suspected some kind of trick. But they changed their minds after talking to Sinon, a Greek warrior whom the Greeks had left behind. Sinon let the Trojans capture him; then he told them that the horse was a peace offering to the goddess Athena. He explained that the Greeks felt they had insulted her and now wanted to express

their sorrow. The Trojans tortured Sinon, but he stuck to his story.

13 Most of the Trojans believed Sinon. One priest, named Laocoön, didn't. "Have no faith in the horse!" he shouted. He then threw a spear at the side of the horse. It made a hollow sound. To silence Laocoön, the gods who favored the Greeks sent two sea serpents to strangle him.

14 Cassandra, the daughter of the Trojan king, also tried to warn her people. But she lived under a curse. Cassandra had once angered the god Apollo. As punishment, Apollo had doomed her always to tell the truth, but never to be believed. So although she saw the deception clearly, no one would listen to her.

15 The Trojans decided to pull the horse inside the city to a spot near the palace. It would make a fine monument, they thought, to their victory over the Greeks. It had been a long time since the Trojans had had anything to celebrate. Now, at last, the siege was over and the war was won—or so they thought. Trojan warriors danced and sang around the horse. They drank wine late into the night. At last, even the guards fell asleep.

16 It was then that the Greeks struck. In truth, they had not sailed away at all. Instead, they had hidden their ships and army behind an nearby island. Now, under the cover of darkness, they gathered outside the walls of Troy. Meanwhile,

Sinon crept over to the wooden horse and opened a secret trap door in the belly of the horse. Out poured the bold Greek warriors who had hidden inside. They opened the gates of Troy and the rest of Melenaus's army streamed in.

17 The battle that then took place was a slaughter. The sleepy Trojans had no chance to regroup. Almost all the Trojans were killed, including the king. The city was completely destroyed—the temples, the altars, all the buildings. Meanwhile, Menelaus captured Helen. He intended to punish her for all the bloodshed she had caused. But he didn't. When he saw her, his heart softened. Realizing he still loved her, he took her back with him to Sparta, where she lived out the rest of her days.

If you have been timed while reading this article, enter your reading time below. Then turn to the Words-per-Minute Table on page 71 and look up your reading speed (words per minute). Enter your reading speed on the graph on page 72.

Reading Time: Lesson 3

_____ : _____
Minutes   Seconds

A Finding the Main Idea

One statement below expresses the main idea of the article. One statement is too general, or too broad. The other statement explains only part of the article; it is too narrow. Label the statements using the following key:

M—Main Idea   **B—Too Broad**   **N—Too Narrow**

_____ 1. In a classic deception, the Greek warriors hid in a giant horse and fooled their enemies, the Trojans, into letting them into their city.

_____ 2. Though the Trojans were suspicious about the giant horse their enemies had left behind, a Greek soldier named Sinon convinced them that the horse was a gift to a goddess.

_____ 3. The Greeks and the Trojans were natural enemies, both wanting control of the Aegean Sea area.

_____ Score 15 points for a correct M answer.

_____ Score 5 points for each correct B or N answer.

_____ **Total Score:** Finding the Main Idea

B Recalling Facts

How well do you remember the facts in the article? Put an X in the box next to the answer that correctly completes each statement about the article.

1. According to legend, the Trojan War began when
   □ a. the Greeks entered Troy in a giant wooden horse.
   □ b. Trojan prince Paris ran away with Helen, the wife of King Menelaus of Sparta.
   □ c. the Greeks put the city of Troy under siege.

2. Paris was aided by the goddess
   □ a. Helen.
   □ b. Agamemnon.
   □ c. Aphrodite.

3. Because Laocoön did not trust the wooden horse, the gods silenced him by
   □ a. sending sea serpents to strangle him.
   □ b. cursing him with never being believed.
   □ c. killing him with an arrow.

4. After the Trojans pulled the horse into their city, they
   □ a. inspected it thoroughly.
   □ b. destroyed it.
   □ c. celebrated late into the night.

5. When Menelaus finally recaptured Helen, he
   □ a. forgave her and took her back to Sparta with him.
   □ b. punished her for the bloodshed she had caused.
   □ c. divorced her.

Score 5 points for each correct answer.

_____ **Total Score:** Recalling Facts

C Making Inferences

When you combine your own experience and information from a text to draw a conclusion that is not directly stated in that text, you are making an inference. Below are five statements that may or may not be inferences based on information in the article. Label the statements using the following key:

C—Correct Inference   F—Faulty Inference

_____ 1. In ancient times, stealing someone's spouse was more acceptable than it is today.

_____ 2. At the time of the Trojan War, the best way to transport soldiers between Sparta and Troy was by ship.

_____ 3. Paris was a kind ruler who thought only of the safety of his citizens.

_____ 4. The Greek soldiers were able to stay quiet for many hours.

_____ 5. Helen was unusually attractive to men.

Score 5 points for each correct answer.

_____ **Total Score:** Making Inferences

D Using Words Precisely

Each numbered sentence below contains an underlined word or phrase from the article. Following the sentence are three definitions. One definition is closest to the meaning of the underlined word. One definition is opposite or nearly opposite. Label those two definitions using the following key. Do not label the remaining definition.

C—Closest   O—Opposite or Nearly Opposite

1. They would have been natural <u>rivals</u> for control of the Aegean Sea.

_____ a. citizens

_____ b. allies

_____ c. competitors

2. With the help of some goddess friends of his own, Menelaus <u>rallied</u> the Greeks to get his wife back.

_____ a. fired up

_____ b. reminded

_____ c. discouraged

3. Thus it was said that Helen was so lovely that "her face <u>launched</u> a thousand ships."

_____ a. sank

_____ b. brought back

_____ c. sent forth

4. Everyone was shocked by such <u>brutal</u> treatment of a fallen foe.

_____ a. kind

_____ b. unfeeling and cruel

_____ c. surprising

5. The sleepy Trojans had no chance to <u>regroup</u>.

_____ a. become confused again

_____ b. organize again

_____ c. go back to sleep

_____ Score 3 points for each correct C answer.

_____ Score 2 points for each correct O answer.

_____ **Total Score:** Using Words Precisely

Enter the four total scores in the spaces below, and add them together to find your Reading Comprehension Score. Then record your score on the graph on page 73.

Score	Question Type	Lesson 3
_____	Finding the Main Idea	
_____	Recalling Facts	
_____	Making Inferences	
_____	Using Words Precisely	
_____	**Reading Comprehension Score**	

Author's Approach

Put an X in the box next to the correct answer.

1. The author uses the first sentence of the article to

☐ a. entertain the reader with a look at a famous battle.

☐ b. describe the qualities of the Greeks.

☐ c. inform the reader of when the Trojan War took place.

2. What does the author mean by this statement about Helen: "her face launched a thousand ships"?

☐ a. A large navy was called upon to rescue her.

☐ b. She christened about 1,000 ships.

☐ c. Her picture was placed on 1,000 ships.

3. What is the author's purpose in writing "The Trojan Horse"?

☐ a. To encourage the reader to study the maps of Greece

☐ b. To entertain the reader with an exciting romance

☐ c. To describe a situation in which deception was used to win a war

4. Which of the following statements from the article best describes the way most Trojans felt when they saw the wooden horse?

☐ a. "Cassandra, the daughter of the Trojan king, also tried to warn her people."

☐ b. "The Trojans tortured Sinon, but he stuck to his story."

☐ c. "At first, the Trojans suspected some kind of trick."

_____ Number of correct answers

Record your personal assessment of your work on the Critical Thinking Chart on page 74.

Summarizing and Paraphrasing

Follow the directions provided for question 1. Put an X in the box next to the correct answer for question 2.

1. Reread paragraph 15 in the article. Below, write a summary of the paragraph in no more than 25 words.

_____

_____

_____

_____

Reread your summary and decide whether it covers the important ideas in the paragraph. Next, decide how to shorten the summary to 15 words or less without leaving out any essential information. Write this summary below.

_____

_____

_____

2. Choose the sentence that correctly restates the following sentence from the article:

"Instead, Patroclus died at the hands of Hector."

☐ a. Instead, Patroclus died near the hands of Hector.

☐ b. Instead, Hector killed Patroclus.

☐ c. Instead, Patroclus and Hector died at the same time.

_____ Number of correct answers

Record your personal assessment of your work on the Critical Thinking Chart on page 74.

Critical Thinking

Put an X in the box next to the correct answer for questions 1 and 3. Follow the directions provided for the other questions.

1. From what the article told about the Trojan War, you can predict that

☐ a. the Greeks and Trojans became trusting friends right after the war.

☐ b. the Greeks and the Trojans distrusted each other for many years after the war.

☐ c. many modern armies have actually tried the trick of the giant wooden horse.

2. Using what you know about Paris and what is told about Achilles in the article, name three ways Paris is similar to and three ways Paris is different from Achilles. Cite the paragraph number(s) where you found details in the article to support your conclusions.

Similarities

_____

_____

_____

Differences

_____

_____

_____

3. What was the effect of Achilles's brutal treatment of Hector's body?

☐ a. The god Apollo leaped into battle on the side of the Trojans.

☐ b. The Trojans refused to fight anymore.

☐ c. The Greeks hid their ships behind a nearby island.

4. Think about cause-effect relationships in the article. Fill in the blanks in the cause-effect chart, drawing from the letters below.

Cause	Effect
Paris ran away with Helen.	_____
Cassandra was cursed.	_____
_____	Neither side could get the upper hand.
_____	The city of Troy was destroyed.

a. Brave men fought on both sides of the war.

b. The Trojans allowed the wooden horse into their city.

c. Menelaus decided tottack Troy.

d. No one believed her even though she told the truth.

5. What did you have to do to answer question 2?

☐ a. find a question (something that is asked)

☐ b. find a purpose (why something is done)

☐ c. find a comparison (how things are the same)

_____ Number of correct answers

Record your personal assessment of your work on the Critical Thinking Chart on page 74.

Personal Response

How do you think Laocoön felt when the Greeks finally came out of the wooden horse?

_____

_____

_____

_____

Self-Assessment

When reading the article, I was having trouble with

_____

_____

_____

_____

CRITICAL THINKING

NEW ERA RIP-OFF

Charles Ponzi, who promised investors easy wealth, lent his name to the pyramid scheme that is still popular today with financial con artists.

I n 1919, Charles Ponzi pulled off one of the most blatant scams in history. Ponzi swindled rich Bostonians out of millions of dollars. His rip-off was a model of simplicity. "Give me your money," Ponzi told people, "and I'll return it in 90 days with 50% interest." Could it be true?

2   Well, in a way, it was true. Ponzi did pay off his first set of investors. But he did it with money he got from his next set of investors. The original clients were thrilled. They didn't realize what Ponzi was doing and they didn't care. All they knew was that they were making money. The word of easy wealth quickly spread. More and more people invested their money with Ponzi. And he kept paying off early investors with money from later investors. In time, Ponzi's bogus financial pyramid collapsed. Since then, all similar scams have become known as "Ponzi schemes."

3   Charles Ponzi may be dead and gone, but his basic scheme is still around. Take the case of John Bennett. In 1989, he set up the Foundation for New Era Philanthropy. Bennett was an expert in

fund-raising techniques. He held prayer breakfasts and served on the board of directors of three charities. Bennett was well known in his home state of Pennsylvania. And he was well liked.

4   Then Bennett began to imitate Ponzi. He promised his clients a 100% return on their money in six months. All the clients had to do was let New Era have their money for those six months. Then a $100,000 deposit would turn into a $200,000 return. Where would the extra $100,000 come from? Bennett claimed it would come from anonymous donors. It seemed like a typical challenge grant. The client is "challenged" to raise a certain amount of money. If the client does so, an unnamed donor matches the amount.

5   Many of Bennett's clients were small Christian colleges or Bible schools. Most had limited resources. If they wanted to stay open, they had to raise funds. So New Era's proposal seemed made to order. The people at Lancaster Bible College in Pennsylvania certainly thought so. "It looked like a great answer to a need we'd been thinking and praying about," said Gilbert Peterson, the head of the school.

6   Like any well-oiled Ponzi scheme, New Era worked like a charm—for a while. Clients did double their money. Bennett soon lured hundreds of clients into New Era. By 1995, there was, as one accountant put it, "an avalanche of money going into [New Era]."

7   Meanwhile, everyone thought Bennett was a swell guy. Like the slick Charlie Ponzi, he was treated as some kind of hero. "The word on the street was that Bennett was a super credible man, impeccable," said one woman. "You'd hear things like, 'Oh, I've known Bennett for 15 years.'"

8   Albert Meyer, however, did not see the hero in John Bennett. Meyer was an accounting teacher at Spring Arbor College in Michigan. He also worked as the school's bookkeeper. One day he noticed that Spring Arbor had invested in New Era. He checked into it. When he read about the double-your-money offer, an alarm went off in his head. "Ponzi! Ponzi!" he thought. But his bosses didn't want to hear about it. "I was told it's tough raising funds," said Meyer later, "and they didn't need my meddling."

9   Still, Meyer kept at it. At last he convinced his superiors to check out New Era in person. But instead of seeing New Era as a rip-off, they came back delighted. New Era had approved their school for $1 million in matching grants over the next three years. "I know you've had concerns," Spring Arbor president Allen Carden told a stunned Meyer, "but we think they're misplaced. The grants are a godsend." So the college kept sending money to New Era. First it sent $400,000. Then it sent half a million dollars. Later the college sent $1 million.

10   Meyer's warnings continued to fall on deaf ears. Other people who had similar

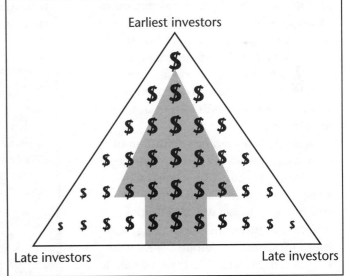

A diagram showing how a Ponzi or pyramid scheme works. Each level of investors provides funds to give profits to previous levels. Eventually, the scheme runs out of investors, and the late investors see no profit.

doubts got the same treatment from their organizations. "When I raised questions about New Era," said one accountant, "I was made to feel like I was swearing in church."

11 Carden's faith in New Era remained unshaken. He proudly displayed a check from New Era for $800,000. That was twice as much as the $400,000 he had sent earlier. The school had plans for a new library. They would start building as soon as the rest of the matching funds rolled in.

12 That never happened. One of New Era's investors sued for a $44.9 million loan that had not been repaid. Then an article in the *Wall Street Journal* exposed the deception for all to see. Bennett had built his house of cards with smoke and mirrors. And now it came crashing down. At the time of its collapse, New Era owed more than $550 million to hundreds of clients. On May 13, 1995, Bennett finally came clean. "I betrayed you all," he tearfully told his staff. "There are no anonymous donors. All I ever wanted was to help people."

13 Bennett had a strange definition of help. Innocent people lost all their hopes and dreams because of his Ponzi scheme. They had put their complete trust in him. One of these people was Jack Crabtree. He was the executive director of Long Island Youth for Christ. His group invested $100,000 in New Era. Crabtree wanted to pray for Bennett. It wasn't easy. "The hardest prayer to get out of my mouth was to pray for John Bennett," he said. "It came out real slow."

14 At his trial, Bennett pleaded "no contest" to 82 counts of fraud. In other words, he did not deny committing the crimes he was accused of. In his defense, his lawyer argued that Bennett suffered "religious fervor." The lawyer explained that Bennett believed that he was on a "mission from God to change the world." A witness reported that Bennett claimed God had talked to him, "telling him what he must do." Judge Edmund Ludwig rejected this line of argument and sentenced Bennett to 12 years in jail.

15 Meanwhile, the schools and colleges Bennett nearly destroyed tried to come back. At Lancaster Bible College, Gilbert Peterson said that this time they would do it the old-fashioned way—"one donor at a time...one dollar at a time."

If you have been timed while reading this article, enter your reading time below. Then turn to the Words-per-Minute Table on page 71 and look up your reading speed (words per minute). Enter your reading speed on the graph on page 72.

Reading Time: Lesson 4

_____ : _____
Minutes   Seconds

A | Finding the Main Idea

One statement below expresses the main idea of the article. One statement is too general, or too broad. The other statement explains only part of the article; it is too narrow. Label the statements using the following key:

M—Main Idea   **B—Too Broad**   **N—Too Narrow**

_____ 1. The Foundation for New Era Philanthropy promised a 100% return on clients' money after only a six-month investment.

_____ 2. The Foundation for New Era Philanthropy caused a number of organizations to lose valuable funds.

_____ 3. Many organizations lost funds by unwisely investing in the Foundation for New Era Philanthropy, a group that promised easy money.

_____ Score 15 points for a correct M answer.

_____ Score 5 points for each correct B or N answer.

_____ **Total Score:** Finding the Main Idea

B | Recalling Facts

How well do you remember the facts in the article? Put an X in the box next to the answer that correctly completes each statement about the article.

1. Ponzi paid off his first set of investors with
   - ☐ a. the money he got from his second set of investors.
   - ☐ b. his life savings.
   - ☐ c. money from the Foundation for New Era Philanthropy.

2. John Bennett claimed that the money he raised for investors came from
   - ☐ a. profits from stocks and bonds.
   - ☐ b. other investors.
   - ☐ c. anonymous donors.

3. When Albert Meyer first suggested that Bennett was not trustworthy,
   - ☐ a. he was fired.
   - ☐ b. he was ignored.
   - ☐ c. his superiors were delighted at his discovery.

4. Bennett's downfall was exposed in
   - ☐ a. the *Wall Street Journal*.
   - ☐ b. the *Washington Post*.
   - ☐ c. the *Los Angeles Times*.

5. Bennett explained to his staff that he began the scheme because he
   - ☐ a. believed it was both legal and profitable for himself and his investors.
   - ☐ b. wanted to make a great deal of money for himself.
   - ☐ c. wanted to help people.

Score 5 points for each correct answer.

_____ **Total Score:** Recalling Facts

C | Making Inferences

When you combine your own experience and information from a text to draw a conclusion that is not directly stated in that text, you are making an inference. Below are five statements that may or may not be inferences based on information in the article. Label the statements using the following key:

C—Correct Inference   **F—Faulty Inference**

_____ 1. Small Christian colleges are supported entirely by government funding.

_____ 2. When a person is found guilty of swindling others out of their money, he or she must pay the money back in full.

_____ 3. The *Wall Street Journal* is a trusted source of information for investors.

_____ 4. At Spring Arbor College, the president, not the bookkeeper, made important financial decisions, such as where to invest their money.

_____ 5. Small Christian colleges and Bible schools usually have large, experienced staffs to manage their money.

Score 5 points for each correct answer.

_____ **Total Score:** Making Inferences

D | Using Words Precisely

Each numbered sentence below contains an underlined word or phrase from the article. Following the sentence are three definitions. One definition is closest to the meaning of the underlined word. One definition is opposite or nearly opposite. Label those two definitions using the following key. Do not label the remaining definition.

C—Closest   **O—Opposite or Nearly Opposite**

1. In time, Ponzi's <u>bogus</u> financial pyramid collapsed.

    _____ a. authentic

    _____ b. fake

    _____ c. famous

2. "The word on the street was that Bennett was a super <u>credible</u> man, impeccable," said one woman.

    _____ a. phony

    _____ b. dedicated

    _____ c. believable

3. "I was told it's tough raising funds," said Meyer later, "and they didn't need my <u>meddling</u>."

    _____ a. unwanted interference

    _____ b. ideas

    _____ c. appropriate interest

4. "I <u>betrayed</u> you all," he tearfully told his staff.

    _____ a. broke faith with

    _____ b. kept promises to

    _____ c. forgot

5. In his defense, his lawyer argued that Bennett suffered "religious fervor."

_____ a. boredom

_____ b. enthusiasm

_____ c. faith

_____ Score 3 points for each correct C answer.

_____ Score 2 points for each correct O answer.

_____ **Total Score:** Using Words Precisely

Enter the four total scores in the spaces below, and add them together to find your Reading Comprehension Score. Then record your score on the graph on page 73.

Score	Question Type	Lesson 4
_____	Finding the Main Idea	
_____	Recalling Facts	
_____	Making Inferences	
_____	Using Words Precisely	
_____	**Reading Comprehension Score**	

Author's Approach

Put an X in the box next to the correct answer.

1. The main purpose of the first two paragraphs is to
   □ a. express an opinion about Charles Ponzi.
   □ b. describe John Bennett.
   □ c. explain the "Ponzi scheme."

2. From statements in the article "New Era Rip-off," you can conclude that the author wants the reader to think that
   □ a. John Bennett was innocent of any crime.
   □ b. Although John Bennett may have been well meaning, his actions harmed many organizations.
   □ c. Bennett was not at all upset about the trouble he caused.

3. In this article, "Bennett had carefully built a house of cards" means
   □ a. Bennett made his money by gambling.
   □ b. Bennett's home was carefully built, using investors' money.
   □ c. Bennett's moneymaking scheme was shaky and unreliable.

4. How is the author's purpose for writing the article expressed in paragraph 13?
   □ a. The paragraph suggests how investor Jack Crabtree feels about Bennett.
   □ b. The paragraph describes how difficult it was for Jack Crabtree to pray for Bennett.
   □ c. The paragraph stresses that innocent people lost their money in Bennett's Ponzi scheme.

_____ Number of correct answers

Record your personal assessment of your work on the Critical Thinking Chart on page 74.

CRITICAL THINKING

Summarizing and Paraphrasing

Follow the directions provided for question 1. Put an X in the box next to the correct answer for the other questions.

1. Complete the following one-sentence summary of the article using the lettered phrases from the phrase bank below. Write the letters on the lines.

> **Phrase Bank:**
> a. how John Bennett used Ponzi's ideas
> b. an explanation of a Ponzi scheme
> c. John Bennett's trial

The article about the Foundation for New Era Philanthropy begins with _____, goes on to explain _____, and ends with _____.

2. Read the statement about the article below. Then read the paraphrase of that statement. Choose the reason that best tells why the paraphrase does not say the same thing as the statement.

Statement: Because many small colleges were desperate for money, they were willing to believe in Bennett's scheme.

Paraphrase: Even though they needed money badly, the small colleges that Bennett targeted were too careful to fall for his scheme.

☐ a. Paraphrase says too much.

☐ b. Paraphrase doesn't say enough.

☐ c. Paraphrase doesn't agree with the statement about the article.

3. Choose the sentence that correctly restates the following sentence from the article:
"Meyer's warnings continued to fall on deaf ears."

☐ a. Meyer worked with deaf students and faculty at his college.

☐ b. No one listened to Meyer's warnings.

☐ c. Meyer's warnings were spoken so softly that they couldn't be heard.

_____ Number of correct answers

Record your personal assessment of your work on the Critical Thinking Chart on page 74.

Critical Thinking

Put an X in the box next to the correct answer for questions 1, 3, and 4. Follow the directions provided for the other questions.

1. Which of the following statements from the article is an opinion rather than a fact?

☐ a. "He held prayer breakfasts and served on the board of directors of three charities."

☐ b. "His rip-off was a model of simplicity."

☐ c. "At his trial, Bennett pleaded 'no contest' to 82 counts of fraud."

2. Choose from the letters below to correctly complete the following statement. Write the letters on the lines.

In the article, _____ and _____ are alike.

a. Charles Ponzi

b. John Bennett

c. Albert Meyer

3. According to Bennett and his lawyer, which of these was a cause of Bennett's engaging in this illegal scheme?

☐ a.   Bennett wanted to make a lot of money for himself.

☐ b.   Bennett wanted to help people and serve God.

☐ c.   Bennett wanted to teach organizations to be more careful with their money.

4. If you were a college president, how could you use the information in the article to manage your funds?

☐ a.   You could remember it when you find a fundraising scheme that seems a little shaky.

☐ b.   You could contact John Bennett when you wanted to make an investment.

☐ c.   You could read the *Wall Street Journal* for more information about the Foundation for New Era Philanthropy.

5. In which paragraphs did you find your information or details to answer question 3?

_____

_____   Number of correct answers

Record your personal assessment of your work on the Critical Thinking Chart on page 74.

Personal Response

A question I would like answered by John Bennett is

_____

_____

_____

_____

Self-Assessment

Which concepts or ideas from the article were difficult to understand?

_____

_____

_____

Which were easy?

_____

_____

_____

FFYONA CAMPBELL

On her world walk, Ffyona Campbell strolls through a pasture of sheep and cows as her journey takes her through Tangier.

Ffyona Campbell had the chance to be a hero. When she set out on her 'round-the-world walk, everyone was rooting for her. For 10 years, she trudged through deserts, over mountains, and across prairies. Her courage and grit made her a role model for young girls everywhere. But in a moment of weakness, Campbell gave it all away. She cheated and she lied. And so instead of being a hero, Campbell ended up disgraced.

2   Ffyona Campbell was born in England in 1967. Her father was a captain in the Royal Navy. His job took the family from place to place. In her first 16 years, Ffyona moved 24 times. She attended 15 different schools. After such a childhood, some people would have craved a calm, settled life. But Ffyona wanted more adventure. She thought she'd find it in long-distance walking.

3   At first, she planned only to walk the length of Great Britain. That she did in 1983. She didn't have much money for the trip, but she hoped sponsors would come forward to help. As she walked, she wore a sweatshirt that said, "SPONSOR ME."

4   Campbell was right. Sponsors *did* offer to cover expenses. These sponsors became even more excited when Campbell announced that she wasn't going to stop with Great Britain; she was going to walk all the way around the world. No woman had ever done that before.

5   Her walk across Great Britain—which she called Stage 1— was 874 miles. When that was behind her, Campbell embarked on Stage 2. This would take her 3,500 miles across the United States. A sponsor, Campbell's Soup Company, agreed to pick up the tab. The company also supplied her with a back-up van carrying food, water, and medical supplies. For her part, Campbell pledged to keep up a pace of 25 miles a day, six days a week.

6   At first, all went well. Campbell left New York and headed for California. For 1,000 miles, she trekked through town after town. In each new place, the press was waiting to greet her and take her photograph. As time passed, though, Campbell had trouble meeting her 25-mile-a-day target. She felt tired, run down. Entering Indiana, she was falling behind schedule. One day, when she felt she couldn't drag herself another step, the driver of her back-up van offered her a ride. Campbell accepted.

7   From that moment on, Campbell was living a lie. Each day she rode a little farther and walked a little less. Soon she was only getting out to walk into towns where press conferences were scheduled. This went on for about a thousand miles. Finally, in New Mexico, Campbell felt stronger. She went back to walking the route.

8   By the time Campbell reached Los Angeles, she was being hailed as a hero. She knew she didn't deserve the praise, but she couldn't bear to admit the truth. So she accepted the honors bestowed upon her. Then she flew home to grapple with her conscience.

9   For months, Campbell tried to figure out what to do. At last, she came up with a plan that she thought she could live with. She would return to America and re-walk the 1,000-mile stretch where she had cheated. Campbell wanted to keep a low profile for this walk. She told only her mother and a few friends what she was doing. And this time, instead of a fancy back-up van, she pushed her equipment in a baby carriage.

10   When Campbell finished this secret walk, she thought she could put the whole ugly mess behind her. She began to look ahead to Stage 3—Australia. She set out across Australia in 1988. It was a journey of 3,200 miles. That made it only slightly shorter than her American walk.

This time, though, Campbell was determined to stick to the rules. This time she would take no rides.

11   As if to prove her worth, Campbell doubled her pace. She tried to average 50 miles a day. That kind of speed made it a grueling trip. Soon she had terrible shinsplints. She also had huge blisters on her feet. Every morning before setting out, she used a needle to drain the blisters. "I was pulling out a liter of pus a week," she said.

Ffyona Campbell celebrates the end of her 11-year walk around the world.

12 After Australia came Africa. This was the most difficult walk of all. Campbell started in Cape Town and headed north. It took her two years to cover the 10,055 miles. Along the way she faced all kinds of perils. Thieves robbed and beat her. Suspicious villagers threw stones at her. Corrupt local officials blocked her path, demanding bribes. In one village, she was arrested as a spy. She also had to deal with the chaos of nations in the midst of civil war. Twice, when rioting broke out, she was evacuated by the Foreign Legion. She then had to wait until the fighting died down before she could continue her walk.

13 Beyond that, the trip held extreme physical challenges. The temperature often topped 100° F. Campbell grew ill with malaria and typhoid. The blisters on her feet became infected. She also developed painful ulcers. Food was often hard to find. At times, Campbell lived on bats, caterpillars, and snails.

14 When Campbell finally completed her African walk, she turned toward home. Stage 5 was a 1,090-mile walk across Europe. Stage 6 was the final leg, with Campbell walking the length of Great Britain to return to her starting point.

15 By the time Campbell neared the finish line, crowds were gathering along the road to cheer her. They smiled and waved and ran alongside her. Campbell had a right to feel proud of what she had done. Even subtracting the thousand miles where she had taken rides, she had still walked over 18,000 miles. No woman had ever gone that far.

16 But Campbell couldn't enjoy her accomplishments. The lies she had told during her American walk still ate away at her. As she later said, "The truth is hard enough to live with, but deceit is even harder. Once you've lied about your achievements, you've created a burden for yourself which you can never, never put down."

17 It pained her to see the trust and respect in her fans' faces. She knew she had betrayed them. When it was announced that her name would go into the *Guinness Book of World Records*, she felt even worse.

18 With her walk over, Campbell was supposed to start writing a book about her experiences. But she couldn't concentrate. She couldn't think of anything except how she had cheated. In time, she became so distraught that she turned to drugs. That's when she realized she had a decision to make. She could destroy her life with drugs or she could admit what she had done.

19 And so in 1996, Campbell went public with her story. She admitted she had cheated during the American leg of her walk. She asked that her name be removed from the *Guinness Book of World Records*. "I shouldn't be remembered as the first woman to walk around the world when I cheated," she told reporters. She went on to tell her fans she was sorry. "To them I owe the biggest apology," she said.

20 After revealing the truth, Campbell was shunned by many people. Family members and close friends stood by her, but others condemned her for her deceit. Still, Campbell had no regrets about revealing the truth. "My lie almost destroyed me," she said. "But once I admitted it and set about putting it right, I discovered that I was out of prison."

If you have been timed while reading this article, enter your reading time below. Then turn to the Words-per-Minute Table on page 71 and look up your reading speed (words per minute). Enter your reading speed on the graph on page 72.

Reading Time: Lesson 5

_____ : _____
Minutes   Seconds

A | Finding the Main Idea

One statement below expresses the main idea of the article. One statement is too general, or too broad. The other statement explains only part of the article; it is too narrow. Label the statements using the following key:

M—Main Idea　　　**B—Too Broad**　　　**N—Too Narrow**

_____ 1. Although Ffyona Campbell claimed that she had walked across the United States, she often had accepted a ride.

_____ 2. Ffyona Campbell was mistakenly given credit for walking around the world, but her conscience forced her to admit that she had cheated.

_____ 3. Ffyona Campbell was the idol of many girls, but she had deceived them.

_____ Score 15 points for a correct M answer.

_____ Score 5 points for each correct B or N answer.

_____ **Total Score:** Finding the Main Idea

B | Recalling Facts

How well do you remember the facts in the article? Put an X in the box next to the answer that correctly completes each statement about the article.

1. Ffyona Campbell's first goal was to walk across
   ☐ a. Europe.
   ☐ b. the United States.
   ☐ c. Great Britain.

2. When Campbell walked across the U.S., she traveled from
   ☐ a. New York to California.
   ☐ b. California to New York.
   ☐ c. Massachusetts to Oregon.

3. Campbell's most physically challenging walk was the one through
   ☐ a. Europe.
   ☐ b. Africa.
   ☐ c. Australia.

4. By the time Campbell stopped walking, she had covered about
   ☐ a. 18,000 miles.
   ☐ b. 50,000 miles.
   ☐ c. 7,500 miles.

5. Campbell said that she owed her biggest apology to
   ☐ a. her family.
   ☐ b. the publishers of the _Guinness Book of World Records_.
   ☐ c. her fans.

_____ Score 5 points for each correct answer.

_____ **Total Score:** Recalling Facts

C **Making Inferences**

When you combine your own experience and information from a text to draw a conclusion that is not directly stated in that text, you are making an inference. Below are five statements that may or may not be inferences based on information in the article. Label the statements using the following key:

C—Correct Inference   **F—Faulty Inference**

_____ 1. Reporters did not follow Campbell on every step of her United States trip.

_____ 2. People in small villages in Africa are not used to seeing white women walking through their towns.

_____ 3. When you walk a long way for a long time, your feet become so tough that you don't have to worry about them.

_____ 4. Campbell was given plenty of supplies throughout her walk through Africa.

_____ 5. The United States is the hardest country to walk across.

Score 5 points for each correct answer.

_____ **Total Score:** Making Inferences

D **Using Words Precisely**

Each numbered sentence below contains an underlined word or phrase from the article. Following the sentence are three definitions. One definition is closest to the meaning of the underlined word. One definition is opposite or nearly opposite. Label those two definitions using the following key. Do not label the remaining definition.

C—Closest   **O—Opposite or Nearly Opposite**

1. Then she flew home to <u>grapple with</u> her conscience.

_____ a. examine

_____ b. soothe

_____ c. wrestle

2. <u>Corrupt</u> local officials blocked her path, demanding bribes.

_____ a. honest

_____ b. crooked

_____ c. curious

3. She also had to deal with the <u>chaos</u> of nations in the midst of civil war.

_____ a. complete confusion

_____ b. armies

_____ c. perfect order

4. In time, she was so <u>distraught</u> that she turned to drugs.

_____ a. calm

_____ b. upset

_____ c. tired

5. After revealing the truth, Campbell was <u>shunned</u> by many people.

_____ a. searched for

_____ b. avoided

_____ c. admired

_____ Score 3 points for each correct C answer.

_____ Score 2 points for each correct O answer.

_____ **Total Score:** Using Words Precisely

Enter the four total scores in the spaces below, and add them together to find your Reading Comprehension Score. Then record your score on the graph on page 73.

Score	Question Type	Lesson 5
_____	Finding the Main Idea	
_____	Recalling Facts	
_____	Making Inferences	
_____	Using Words Precisely	
_____	**Reading Comprehension Score**	

Author's Approach

Put an X in the box next to the correct answer.

1. The main purpose of the first paragraph is to

☐ a. persuade readers to tell the truth always.

☐ b. give an overview of the article that is beginning.

☐ c. explain why Ffyona Campbell cheated.

2. Which of the following statements from the article best describes Campbell's walk through Africa?

☐ a. "In each new place, the press was waiting to greet her and take her photograph."

☐ b. "As she walked, she wore a sweatshirt that said, "SPONSOR ME.""

☐ c. "At times, Campbell lived on bats, caterpillars, and snails."

3. In this article, "Campbell wanted to keep a low profile for this walk" means that on this walk

☐ a. Campbell wanted to avoid mountainous areas.

☐ b. Campbell didn't want to spend much money.

☐ c. Campbell didn't want people paying attention to her.

_____ Number of correct answers

Record your personal assessment of your work on the Critical Thinking Chart on page 74.

CRITICAL THINKING

Summarizing and Paraphrasing

Put an X in the box next to the correct answer for questions 1 and 3. Follow the directions provided for the other question.

1. Below are summaries of the article. Choose the summary that says all the most important things about the article but in the fewest words.

☐ a. Ffyona Campbell's name was printed in the *Guinness Book of World Records* as being the first woman to walk around the world, but she really had cheated by riding about 1,000 miles of the journey in a van when she was in the United States.

☐ b. Though no one knew that she had cheated and had not walked around the world as she had claimed to, Ffyona Campbell confessed to her lie to soothe her conscience.

☐ c. After Ffyona Campbell admitted that she cheated, her name was removed from the *Guinness Book of World Records*.

2. Reread paragraph 7 in the article. Below, write a summary of the paragraph in no more than 25 words.

_____

_____

_____

_____

Reread your summary and decide whether it covers the important ideas in the paragraph. Next, decide how to shorten the summary to 15 words or less without leaving out any essential information. Write this summary below.

_____

_____

3. Choose the best one-sentence paraphrase for the following sentence from the article:

"And so in 1996, Campbell went public with her story."

☐ a. In 1996, Campbell let the public know what had really happened.

☐ b. In 1996, Campbell let reporters follow her on her walking tour.

☐ c. In 1996, Campbell published the story of her life.

_____ Number of correct answers

Record your personal assessment of your work on the Critical Thinking Chart on page 74.

Critical Thinking

Put an X in the box next to the correct answer for questions 1 and 2. Follow the directions provided for the other questions.

1. Which of the following statements from the article is an opinion rather than a fact?

☐ a. "Campbell had a right to feel proud of what she had done."

☐ b. "It took her two years to cover the 10,055 miles."

☐ c. "Campbell grew ill with malaria and typhoid."

2. Judging by Campbell's actions as told in this article, you can predict that

☐ a. Campbell will never walk anywhere again.

☐ b. Campbell will never try to deceive her fans again.

☐ c. Campbell will walk around the world at least one more time.

3. Choose from the letters below to correctly complete the following statement. Write the letters on the lines.

On the positive side, _____, but on the negative side _____.

   a.   Campbell actually did walk around the world

   b.   Campbell lied about her feat during the U.S. leg of the trip

   c.   Campbell doubled her pace during the Australia leg of the trip

4. Read paragraph 11. Then choose from the letters below to correctly complete the following statement. Write the letters on the lines.

According to paragraph 11, _____ happened because _____.

   a.   Campbell doubled her pace to 50 miles per day

   b.   Campbell enjoyed her trip through Australia

   c.   Campbell got shinsplints and blisters

5. What did you have to do to answer question 2?

  ☐ a.   find a list (a number of things)

  ☐ b.   find a description (how something looks)

  ☐ c.   make a prediction (what might happen next)

_____ Number of correct answers

Record your personal assessment of your work on the Critical Thinking Chart on page 74.

Personal Response

Describe a time when you told a lie or let someone believe a lie.

_____

_____

_____

_____

Self-Assessment

From reading this article, I have learned

_____

_____

_____

_____

CRITICAL THINKING

DAVID WILLIAMS
Impostor

O n the night of July 17, 1996, TWA Flight 800 fell out of the sky, killing 230 people. The plane plunged into the sea off the coast of Long Island, New York. Rescue workers rushed to the Coast Guard command center at East Moriches. One of them, David Williams, wore the uniform of an Army lieutenant colonel. Williams raced up to a police checkpoint. There a guard asked him for identification. Williams grabbed his ID card and shoved it in the man's face. "Let's cut the [nonsense]," he barked. The guard quickly waved him through.

2 Williams then took over the task of directing the landing of helicopters. With just a pair of red flashlights, he guided dozens of helicopters to the right landing spot. It was a frantic scene. Rescue workers were flooding in. One helicopter carried the governor of New York. Another brought the mayor of New York City. And a third carried the FBI agent in charge of investigating the crash. Williams got them all safely to the proper place. He seemed to know just what he was doing. Peggy Foy, a Civil Air Patrol worker, said he

David Williams was present at the scene of the TWA Flight 800 disaster. Here, a large section of fuselage from the downed aircraft is lifted to shore.

acted "very professionally." But things were not quite what they seemed to be.

3   For two and a half days, Colonel Williams continued to do his job. But doubts about him soon arose. A few of the chopper pilots grumbled that his landing signals were outdated. There were other clues as well. Williams wore an olive-drab flight jacket with Army Airborne patches. That seemed normal. But, strangely, he also wore an Air Force medical insignia. Williams couldn't be in the Army *and* the Air Force at the same time.

4   Finally, on July 20, the police checked William's identification. This time they took a closer look. His ID was a fake. As things turned out, Williams was not an army officer. In fact, he had never even been in the army. News reports of his impersonation alerted other people to Williams. Within a week, the rest of his made-up life came crashing down.

5   Police discovered that David Williams was an accomplished impostor. His two best roles were doctor and army officer. In 1992, he became "Doctor David Williams." He took a job as a health teacher for the Long Island Minority AIDS Coalition. Three years later, he found similar work with another agency.

6   Williams liked playing doctor. Each day he came to work in a white lab coat with a stethoscope dangling from his neck. He wrote prescriptions. He gave medical advice. And he spent hours talking to patients with AIDS. Williams did not use the role to get rich. Rather, he seemed to have a real desire to do good. "If anything," said one health worker, "he would offer up his time for things like health fairs…where he wasn't paid."

7   On weekends, meanwhile, Williams turned into "Colonel David Williams." He went to McGuire Air Force Base in New Jersey. There he gave a class on medical training. Williams also worked with an inspection team that made sure army units were ready to go to war.

8   No one suspected a thing. Williams was good at what he did. "He was friendly, very outgoing, and you would never know he was not a doctor or [an] officer," said Sergeant Donna Gauze. She worked with Williams at McGuire. "He was very, very specific about what procedures had to be followed."

9   In real life, Williams was the son of a New Jersey car dealer. He never graduated from college, but did spend five years attending Seton Hall University. Along the way, he picked up enough medical knowledge to fool people. And he was a good forger. To get his job at McGuire, Williams wrote his own transfer orders from Scott Air Force Base in Illinois. One official at McGuire was later asked if he was embarrassed that Williams had been accepted so easily. "Are we embarrassed? No," said Art Covello. "This guy came with credentials. His face became known."

10   Williams liked to flirt with exposure by telling tall tales. He created a whole new life story for himself. And he added chapters as he went along. Many times he told friends and colleagues that he had to go on a "secret mission." He told

Wreckage from Flight 800 is unloaded in Hampton Bay, New York.

harrowing war stories. For instance, he said he had won a Purple Heart for being wounded in a Somali desert. No one bothered to check up on him.

11   By his own fake credentials, he was overqualified for the jobs he held. After all, he was hired as a health teacher, not as a doctor. He was once asked about this. Williams had a ready answer. He suffered from "post-traumatic stress disorder." He said it came from his service in the Persian Gulf War. One day he had been walking through an Iraqi village which had just been bombed. There were dead and wounded victims lying all around. Suddenly, one wounded Iraqi soldier reached up and stabbed him in the leg. Since then, Williams explained, he couldn't stomach the sight of blood. So he had stopped practicing medicine and had become a teacher. However, he still kept the title of "Doctor Williams."

12   On August 9, 1996, David Williams was indicted by a grand jury. He was charged with eleven counts of posing as a doctor. In that role, he had ordered $87,000 in Medicaid services. At his trial, it was learned that all those expenses were sound. In other words, any real doctor would have ordered the same services. Still, it is against the law to do what he did without a license.

13   In the end, David Williams pleaded guilty to one count of "unauthorized practice of a profession." He was sentenced to five years probation and six months in jail. He could have gotten 35 to 86 years. But he had done no harm. And it was clear that he had serious mental health problems. Judge John Vaughn ordered him to have psychiatric testing. Even his own lawyer, said, "[These impersonations] are not the actions of a normal human being."

14   For those who knew Williams, word of his troubles came as a total shock. Most had come to respect and even love him. He had a gentle touch and was always ready to support a friend. But there was clearly a side to David Williams that most people didn't know. Sorraya Sampson had hired him to work for the AIDS Coalition. After his downfall, she said, "Now, in many ways, I feel as though I never knew David at all." 🍃

If you have been timed while reading this article, enter your reading time below. Then turn to the Words-per-Minute Table on page 71 and look up your reading speed (words per minute). Enter your reading speed on the graph on page 72.

Reading Time: Lesson 6

_____ : _____

Minutes   Seconds

A | Finding the Main Idea

One statement below expresses the main idea of the article. One statement is too general, or too broad. The other statement explains only part of the article; it is too narrow. Label the statements using the following key:

M—Main Idea   **B—Too Broad**   **N—Too Narrow**

_____ 1. David Williams was a man of many talents whose goal was simply to help others.

_____ 2. David Williams presented himself as an expert in many fields, but he was lying about his abilities.

_____ 3. While David Williams was pretending to be a doctor, he ordered about $87,000 worth of Medicaid services, all of them necessary.

_____ Score 15 points for a correct M answer.

_____ Score 5 points for each correct B or N answer.

_____ **Total Score:** Finding the Main Idea

B | Recalling Facts

How well do you remember the facts in the article? Put an X in the box next to the answer that correctly completes each statement about the article.

1. At the site of the crash of Flight 800, David Williams posed as
   ☐ a. an Air Force doctor.
   ☐ b. a Coast Guard official.
   ☐ c. an Army lieutenant colonel.

2. This clue alerted police to Williams's deception at the crash site:
   ☐ a. he wore both Army and Air Force symbols.
   ☐ b. he didn't perform his duties safely.
   ☐ c. he didn't know how to salute properly.

3. Williams claimed that he lost his ability to handle the sight of blood when
   ☐ a. he had been forced to kill someone in battle.
   ☐ b. he had been stabbed by a wounded Iraqi soldier.
   ☐ c. his father died in a bloody car crash.

4. Williams claimed that the U.S. government had awarded him the
   ☐ a. Presidential Medal of Freedom.
   ☐ b. Bronze Star.
   ☐ c. Purple Heart.

5. Williams was sentenced to
   ☐ a. five years probation and six months in jail.
   ☐ b. five years in jail.
   ☐ c. five years in jail and six months probation.

Score 5 points for each correct answer.

_____ **Total Score:** Recalling Facts

C | Making Inferences

When you combine your own experience and information from a text to draw a conclusion that is not directly stated in that text, you are making an inference. Below are five statements that may or may not be inferences based on information in the article. Label the statements using the following key:

C—Correct Inference   F—Faulty Inference

_____ 1. If David Williams had learned up-to-date landing signals and worn the correct insignia on his uniform, he might not have been discovered as an impostor.

_____ 2. Williams knew more than the average person about the practice of medicine.

_____ 3. When a plane crash results in many deaths, various government officials assemble at the site.

_____ 4. David Williams believed that teachers see blood on a regular basis.

_____ 5. A doctor completes much more training than a health teacher does.

Score 5 points for each correct answer.

_____ **Total Score:** Making Inferences

D | Using Words Precisely

Each numbered sentence below contains an underlined word or phrase from the article. Following the sentence are three definitions. One definition is closest to the meaning of the underlined word. One definition is opposite or nearly opposite. Label those two definitions using the following key. Do not label the remaining definition.

C—Closest   O—Opposite or Nearly Opposite

1. Police discovered that David Williams was an accomplished impostor.

_____ a. pretender

_____ b. entertainer

_____ c. honest person

2. "This guy came with credentials."

_____ a. papers that question one's abilities

_____ b. friends

_____ c. references

3. He told harrowing war stories.

_____ a. chilling

_____ b. comforting

_____ c. many

4. On August 9, 1996, David Williams was indicted by a grand jury.

_____ a. excused

_____ b. charged with a crime

_____ c. identified

5. In the end, David Williams pleaded guilty to one count of "<u>unauthorized</u> practice of a profession."

_____ a. unwritten

_____ b. blessed by authorities

_____ c. not approved by authorities

_____ Score 3 points for each correct C answer.

_____ Score 2 points for each correct O answer.

_____ **Total Score:** Using Words Precisely

Enter the four total scores in the spaces below, and add them together to find your Reading Comprehension Score. Then record your score on the graph on page 73.

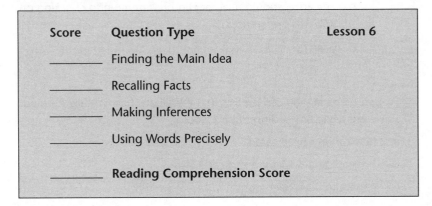

Score	Question Type	Lesson 6
_____	Finding the Main Idea	
_____	Recalling Facts	
_____	Making Inferences	
_____	Using Words Precisely	
_____	**Reading Comprehension Score**	

Author's Approach

Put an X in the box next to the correct answer.

1. What is the author's purpose in writing "David Williams: Impostor"?

☐ a. To encourage the reader to stay in school

☐ b. To inform the reader about an interesting character

☐ c. To convey a cheerful mood

2. From the statements below, choose those that you believe the author would agree with.

☐ a. David Williams should be allowed to continue with his practice of medicine even though he has no license.

☐ b. David Williams was an evil person who should be punished to the full extent of the law.

☐ c. David Williams was a good-hearted person with mental problems.

3. The author tells this story mainly by

☐ a. retelling personal experiences.

☐ b. comparing different topics.

☐ c. telling different stories about the same topic.

_____ Number of correct answers

Record your personal assessment of your work on the Critical Thinking Chart on page 74.

Summarizing and Paraphrasing

Follow the directions provided for question 1. Put an X in the box next to the correct answer for the other questions.

1. Look for the important ideas and events in paragraphs 3 and 4. Summarize those paragraphs in one or two sentences.

_____

_____

_____

2. Read the statement about the article below. Then read the paraphrase of that statement. Choose the reason that best tells why the paraphrase does not say the same thing as the statement.

   Statement:　David Williams could always be counted on to give his time to care for his patients.

   Paraphrase:　Each day, David Williams willingly gave his time to write prescriptions, give medical advice, and talk to AIDS patients, even though he had no license.

   ☐　a.　Paraphrase says too much.

   ☐　b.　Paraphrase doesn't say enough.

   ☐　c.　Paraphrase doesn't agree with the statement about the article.

3. Choose the sentence that correctly restates the following sentence from the article: "Williams liked to flirt with exposure by telling tall tales."

   ☐　a.　Williams had plenty of female friends who enjoyed his tall tales.

   ☐　b.　Williams enjoyed telling tall tales to entertain his friends.

   ☐　c.　Williams liked to tell attention-getting lies, risking the possibility that someone would check on his details and uncover the truth.

_____　Number of correct answers

Record your personal assessment of your work on the Critical Thinking Chart on page 74.

Critical Thinking

Follow the directions provided for questions 1 and 3. Put an X in the box next to the correct answer for the other questions.

1. For each statement below, write O if it expresses an opinion and write F if it expresses a fact.

   _____　a.　No one should feel sorry for a person who impersonates a doctor.

   _____　b.　The army should have paid more attention to checking on Williams's references.

   _____　c.　Williams claimed that he had been wounded in the Somali desert.

2. From the article, you can predict that if Williams had actually harmed someone while pretending to be a doctor,

   ☐　a.　he wouldn't have cared.

   ☐　b.　he would have blamed someone else.

   ☐　c.　he would have been punished more severely.

3. Choose from the letters below to correctly complete the following statement. Write the letters on the lines.

   On the positive side, _____, but on the negative side _____.

   a. Williams wore both Army and Air Force insignias at the same time

   b. Williams told people lies about himself

   c. Williams helped plenty of sick people

4. How is being an impostor related to the profession of acting?

   ☐ a. In both, you pretend to be someone you aren't.

   ☐ b. In both, you put people's lives in danger.

   ☐ c. In both, you make a great deal of money.

5. In which paragraph did you find your information or details to answer question 2?

   _____

_____ Number of correct answers

Record your personal assessment of your work on the Critical Thinking Chart on page 74.

Personal Response

I wonder why

_____

_____

_____

_____

Self-Assessment

One of the things I did best when reading this article was

_____

_____

_____

_____

I believe I did this well because

_____

_____

_____

_____

MARIE HILLEY
The Perfect Wife and Mother

Everyone thought Marie Hilley loved her husband. She and Frank had been married for 24 years. They had a nice home, steady jobs, and two healthy children. It seemed like a terrible twist of fate that Frank suddenly became sick and died at age 45. Folks in Anniston, Alabama, felt sorry for the wife he left behind. In time, however, they would learn a shocking secret. Marie Hilly was not the grieving widow she appeared to be. In fact, she was a cold-blooded killer who had murdered her husband by feeding him rat poison.

2   Marie Hilley was a small, pretty woman. The only child of two mill workers, she was the first in her family to finish high school. After she married Frank, she settled into her life as wife and mother. She also worked as a secretary for some of the biggest businesses in town. Everyone who met Marie was struck by her charm. They described her as sweet, gracious, demure.

3   Underneath the charm, though, lay a calculating coldness. Marie wanted more money than she and Frank made. Her thoughts turned to Frank's insurance policy. If he died, she would get $31,000.

Marie Hilley's deception spanned several years. For a time, she lived in a small town in New England under an assumed name.

While that might not seem like a great deal of money, it was three times the annual income of many people in Anniston. Apparently, Marie found it an irresistible sum.

4   Sometime in 1975, Marie got hold of some rat poison. It contained arsenic, which is deadly to humans. In small doses, arsenic brings on intense stomach pain along with vomiting. In larger doses, it attacks muscles and nerves. It causes tingling in the hands and feet, then paralysis, then death.

5   Arsenic poisoning is easy to spot if doctors are looking for it. One quick look at a victim's fingernails gives it away. As arsenic builds up in the body, it forms telltale white lines under the fingernails. But if doctors are not looking for it, the symptoms look like many other ailments. In Frank's case, doctors at first thought he had the flu. His stomach hurt and he couldn't hold down any food.

6   For a week, Marie played the role of faithful nurse, bringing him food and water. She also gave him a mysterious injection that she said the doctor had authorized. (He hadn't.) But instead of getting better, Frank got worse. Marie took him to the hospital, where he died two days later. Doctors ruled the cause of death to be hepatitis, a liver disease.

7   Frank had been dead less than a week when Marie filed a claim for the $31,000 in insurance money. She went through the money fast. She bought cars, furniture, and mounds of clothes. By 1978, she was broke. That year, Marie took out a $25,000 life insurance policy on her teenage daughter, Carol. And several months after that, Carol began to exhibit some of the same troubling symptoms that had plagued her father.

8   Starting in April 1979, Carol felt sharp pains in her stomach. She vomited for hours at a time. Marie took her to doctors, but they could find nothing wrong. Marie gave Carol an injection, telling her it would help calm her stomach. Soon after that, Carol's hands and feet began to feel numb. Marie took her back to the doctors. Still, none of them could figure out what was wrong.

9   In August, baffled doctors suggested the problem was all in Carol's head. Marie promptly admitted her daughter to a mental hospital. Still, the teenager continued to suffer. Her weight had dropped to a dangerously low level. She was so weak she could no longer walk. Almost every day, Marie brought Carol's favorite food from home, urging her to eat. After every meal, though, Carol seemed to get worse.

10   By September, at least one doctor suspected Carol had been poisoned. He thought she might have been accidentally exposed to something toxic. The doctor told Marie his fears. He said he planned to run some new tests. Before he had the chance, Marie checked Carol out of that hospital. A few days later, with her

Marie Hilley is handcuffed as she is escorted from federal court in 1983.

daughter near death, Marie took Carol to a different hospital.

11 Marie probably thought Carol would die quickly at this new hospital. Instead, she lived. And it was at this hospital that the truth surfaced. Carol had mammoth amounts of arsenic in her system.

12 By then, Marie had been out of money for months. Most of the checks she had written had bounced. One company complained to the police. In September 1979, Marie was arrested for passing bad checks. So she was already in jail when police found out about the arsenic.

13 Marie denied doing anything wrong. She tried to make police believe Carol had poisoned herself. She could not explain why she had a pillbox of arsenic in her purse and another box of it at home. Then police dug up Frank Hilley's body. They found that he had not died of hepatitis. Rather, his body was full of arsenic.

14 Marie was running out of excuses. So she did the only thing she could think of: she ran. While she was out on bail awaiting trial, she disappeared. For three years, no one had a clue what had happened to her.

15 In some ways, Marie's three years in hiding were even more bizarre than her life in Alabama. She fled to Florida, where she met a man named John Homan. She told him her name was Robbi Hanson. Homan fell deeply in love with her. The two of them moved to a small town in New Hampshire. They both found jobs in the area and soon got married.

16 After a while, though, "Robbi" told Homan she was not feeling well. Actually, she said, she was very sick—possibly dying. She then told Homan she needed to visit her twin sister Teri in Texas to wrap up some family business. Homan hated to see his wife leave. But he promised he would be waiting for her when she got back.

17 A month after "Robbi" left, Homan got a call from a woman claiming to be Robbi's twin sister Teri. There was, of course, no "Robbi" and no "Teri." Both of them were characters made up by Marie Hilley. Over the phone, Marie told Homan that "Robbi" had died. Speaking as "Teri," she said she was coming to New Hampshire to console him.

18 When Marie returned to New Hampshire as "Teri," she had lost 30 pounds. She had dyed her dark hair blond. She had also changed some of her habits. She smoked a different brand of cigarette. And while "Robbi" loved to read, "Teri" was a big TV-watcher.

19 Homan was surprised to see how much "Teri" looked like his dead wife. But he figured that wasn't unusual for twins. He accepted "Teri" into his home and introduced her to his friends.

20 Marie might have gone on living as Teri if not for a mix-up by police. Local officers mistook Marie for another criminal who was in the area. They brought her to the police station for questioning. There, she shocked everyone by admitting her true identity.

21 In 1983, Marie Hilley was brought back to Alabama and put on trial for her crimes. The jury quickly found her guilty. She was sentenced to life in prison. But Marie Hilley's story did not end there. Four years after her trial, she escaped from prison. She was found four days later, outside a house in her hometown. She was slumped over in the rain and mud, purple with cold. She was rushed to the hospital, but died of hypothermia and heart failure.

22 When Marie Hilley died, many people were left shaking their heads in bewilderment. It was hard to believe that a woman would kill her husband for a few thousand dollars. It was harder still to imagine a mother deliberately poisoning her own child. Marie's behavior in New Hampshire was another puzzle. It made sense that she created the character of "Robbi." She was, after all, a fugitive who needed a new identity. But why did she decide to kill off "Robbi" and become "Teri?"

23 We will never know the inner workings of Marie Hilley's mind. But perhaps her friend Elmer Williamson summed it up best. He said, "Everyone has secrets. But Marie had more than most. All kinds of terrible secrets gnawing inside her." ◢

If you have been timed while reading this article, enter your reading time below. Then turn to the Words-per-Minute Table on page 71 and look up your reading speed (words per minute). Enter your reading speed on the graph on page 72.

Reading Time: Lesson 7

_____ : _____

Minutes   Seconds

A | Finding the Main Idea

One statement below expresses the main idea of the article. One statement is too general, or too broad. The other statement explains only part of the article; it is too narrow. Label the statements using the following key:

M—Main Idea   **B—Too Broad**   **N—Too Narrow**

_____   1. No one understands why model wife and mother Marie Hilley poisoned her family and then created a new identity for herself.

_____   2. Because young Carol Hilley had clearly been poisoned, officials dug up Frank Hilley's body to examine it for signs of arsenic poisoning.

_____   3. Marie Hilley's life remains a mystery to everyone who knew and loved her.

_____   Score 15 points for a correct M answer.

_____   Score 5 points for each correct B or N answer.

_____   **Total Score:** Finding the Main Idea

B | Recalling Facts

How well do you remember the facts in the article? Put an X in the box next to the answer that correctly completes each statement about the article.

1. The symptoms of Frank Hilley's illness included
   ☐ a. stomach pain.
   ☐ b. double vision.
   ☐ c. joint stiffness.

2. Police believe that Marie killed her husband because
   ☐ a. voices in her head ordered her to kill him.
   ☐ b. he had abused her and their children.
   ☐ c. she wanted the insurance money.

3. When police found out about Carol's arsenic poisoning, Marie was already in jail for
   ☐ a. stealing from the company where she worked.
   ☐ b. passing bad checks.
   ☐ c. trying to poison her daughter.

4. Posing as Robbi Hanson, Marie told her husband she had to visit Texas because
   ☐ a. her twin sister was dying.
   ☐ b. she needed to complete family business.
   ☐ c. she needed a vacation.

5. After Marie escaped from prison, police found her
   ☐ a. dead in an empty warehouse.
   ☐ b. walking around dazed in a town in Texas.
   ☐ c. very ill outside a house in her hometown.

Score 5 points for each correct answer.

_____   **Total Score:** Recalling Facts

C | Making Inferences

When you combine your own experience and information from a text to draw a conclusion that is not directly stated in that text, you are making an inference. Below are five statements that may or may not be inferences based on information in the article. Label the statements using the following key:

C—Correct Inference   **F—Faulty Inference**

_____ 1. Marie Hilley was constantly observed in prison.

_____ 2. Doctors don't expect typical middle-class women to poison their husbands.

_____ 3. The injections that Marie gave her husband and daughter had nothing to do with their illness.

_____ 4. Marie was skillful in covering up her true feelings.

_____ 5. When patients change hospitals, their records always travel along with them.

Score 5 points for each correct answer.

_____ **Total Score:** Making Inferences

D | Using Words Precisely

Each numbered sentence below contains an underlined word or phrase from the article. Following the sentence are three definitions. One definition is closest to the meaning of the underlined word. One definition is opposite or nearly opposite. Label those two definitions using the following key. Do not label the remaining definition.

C—Closest   **O—Opposite or Nearly Opposite**

1. They described her as sweet, gracious, <u>demure</u>.

_____ a. attractive

_____ b. reserved

_____ c. extremely outgoing

2. And several months after that, Carol began to exhibit some of the same troubling symptoms that had <u>plagued</u> her father.

_____ a. pleased

_____ b. hidden from

_____ c. tormented

3. Carol had <u>mammoth</u> amounts of arsenic in her system.

_____ a. huge

_____ b. tiny

_____ c. surprising

4. Speaking as "Teri," she said she was coming to New Hampshire to <u>console</u> him.

_____ a. irritate

_____ b. meet

_____ c. comfort

5. When Marie Hilley died, many people were left shaking their heads in <u>bewilderment</u>.

_____ a. anger

_____ b. puzzlement

_____ c. understanding

_____ Score 3 points for each correct C answer.

_____ Score 2 points for each correct O answer.

_____ **Total Score:** Using Words Precisely

Enter the four total scores in the spaces below, and add them together to find your Reading Comprehension Score. Then record your score on the graph on page 73.

Score	Question Type	Lesson 7
_____	Finding the Main Idea	
_____	Recalling Facts	
_____	Making Inferences	
_____	Using Words Precisely	
_____	**Reading Comprehension Score**	

Author's Approach

Put an X in the box next to the correct answer.

1. The author uses the first sentence of the article to

☐ a. entertain the reader with a story of love and romance.

☐ b. describe the way Marie Hilley appeared to her neighbors.

☐ c. compare Marie Hilley and her husband.

2. What does the author mean by the statement "She went through the money fast"?

☐ a. She spent the money quickly.

☐ b. She looked at the money immediately.

☐ c. She counted the money quickly.

3. What does the author imply by saying "Almost every day, Marie brought Carol's favorite food from home, urging her to eat. After every meal, though, Carol seemed to get worse."

☐ a. Carol felt sick because she hated her mother.

☐ b. Something in the food was making Carol sick.

☐ c. Marie was a kind and caring mother.

4. Choose the statement below that best describes the author's position in paragraph 6.

☐ a. The doctors caring for her husband were careless.

☐ b. Marie tried her best to care for her husband during his illness.

☐ c. Marie was being dishonest all during her husband's illness.

_____ Number of correct answers

Record your personal assessment of your work on the Critical Thinking Chart on page 74.

Summarizing and Paraphrasing

Follow the directions provided for question 1. Put an X in the box next to the correct answer for question 2.

1. Reread paragraph 10 in the article. Below, write a summary of the paragraph in no more than 25 words.

_____

_____

_____

_____

Reread your summary and decide whether it covers the important ideas in the paragraph. Next, decide how to shorten the summary to 15 words or less without leaving out any essential information. Write this summary below.

_____

_____

_____

2. Choose the best one-sentence paraphrase for the following sentence from the article:

"In August, baffled doctors suggested the problem was all in Carol's head."

☐ a. The doctors decided that Carol's skull had been damaged.

☐ b. The doctors thought that Carol might be mentally ill.

☐ c. The doctors were sure that Carol was imagining her illness.

_____ Number of correct answers

Record your personal assessment of your work on the Critical Thinking Chart on page 74.

Critical Thinking

Put an X in the box next to the correct answer for questions 1, 2, and 4. Follow the directions provided for the other questions.

1. Which of the following statements from the article is an opinion rather than a fact?

☐ a. "Starting in April 1979, Carol felt sharp pains in her stomach."

☐ b. "After a while, though, 'Robbi' told Homan she was not feeling well."

☐ c. "In some ways, Marie's three years in hiding were even more bizarre than her life in Alabama."

2. From the article, you can predict that if doctors hadn't found the arsenic in Carol's body,

☐ a. in time, Carol probably would have recovered.

☐ b. police would not have dug up Frank Hilley's body.

☐ c. Carol would have lived for many years in a mental hospital.

3. Choose from the letters below to correctly complete the following statement. Write the letters on the lines.

According to the article, _____ caused _____ to _____.

a. get sick and die

b. arsenic poisoning

c. Frank Hilley

4. Of the following theme categories, which would this story fit into?

☐ a. reality-based stories

☐ b. tales of courage

☐ c. fantasies

5. What did you have to do to answer question 4?

☐ a. find an opinion (what someone thinks about something)

☐ b. find a comparison (how things are the same)

☐ c. draw a conclusion (a sensible statement based on the text and your experience)

_____ Number of correct answers

Record your personal assessment of your work on the Critical Thinking Chart on page 74.

Personal Response

If I were the author, I would add

_____

_____

_____

because

_____

_____

_____

_____

Self-Assessment

I was confused on question # _____ in section _____

because _____

_____

_____

_____

CRITICAL THINKING

Compare and Contrast

Think about the articles you have read in Unit One. Pick the four deceptions you thought were the most fascinating and write their titles in the first column of the chart below. Use information you learned from the articles to fill in the empty boxes of the chart.

Title	What part of the deception was most daring?	As you read, how did you feel toward the people who were deceiving others?	How was the life of each deceiver changed by his or her trickery?

The deception that seemed to cause the least hardship for its victims was _____. I chose this one because _____

_____

_____

Words-per-Minute Table

Unit One

Directions: If you were timed while reading an article, refer to the Reading Time you recorded in the box at the end of the article. Use this words-per-minute table to determine your reading speed for that article. Then plot your reading speed on the graph on page 72.

Lesson No. of Words	Sample 906	1 991	2 986	3 1161	4 1063	5 1260	6 1093	7 1387	Seconds
1:30	604	660	657	774	709	840	729	925	90
1:40	544	595	592	697	638	756	656	832	100
1:50	494	541	538	633	580	687	596	757	110
2:00	453	495	493	581	532	630	547	694	120
2:10	418	457	455	536	491	582	504	640	130
2:20	388	425	423	498	456	540	468	594	140
2:30	362	396	394	464	425	504	437	555	150
2:40	340	372	370	435	399	473	410	520	160
2:50	320	350	348	410	375	445	386	490	170
3:00	302	330	329	387	354	420	364	462	180
3:10	286	313	311	367	336	398	345	438	190
3:20	272	297	296	348	319	378	328	416	200
3:30	259	283	282	332	304	360	312	396	210
3:40	247	270	269	317	290	344	298	378	220
3:50	236	259	257	303	277	329	285	362	230
4:00	227	248	247	290	266	315	273	347	240
4:10	217	238	237	279	255	302	262	333	250
4:20	209	229	228	268	245	291	252	320	260
4:30	201	220	219	258	236	280	243	308	270
4:40	194	212	211	249	228	270	234	297	280
4:50	187	205	204	240	220	261	226	287	290
5:00	181	198	197	232	213	252	219	277	300
5:10	175	192	191	225	206	244	212	268	310
5:20	170	186	185	218	199	236	205	260	320
5:30	165	180	179	211	193	229	199	252	330
5:40	160	175	174	205	188	222	193	245	340
5:50	155	170	169	199	182	216	187	238	350
6:00	151	165	164	194	177	210	182	231	360
6:10	147	161	160	188	172	204	177	225	370
6:20	143	156	156	183	168	199	173	219	380
6:30	139	152	152	179	164	194	168	213	390
6:40	136	149	148	174	159	189	164	208	400
6:50	133	145	144	170	156	184	160	203	410
7:00	129	142	141	166	152	180	156	198	420
7:10	126	138	138	162	148	176	153	194	430
7:20	124	135	134	158	145	172	149	189	440
7:30	121	132	131	155	142	168	146	185	450
7:40	118	129	129	151	139	164	143	181	460
7:50	116	127	126	148	136	161	140	177	470
8:00	113	124	123	145	133	158	137	173	480

Minutes and Seconds

Plotting Your Progress: Reading Speed

Unit One

Directions: If you were timed while reading an article, write your words-per-minute rate for that article in the box under the number of the lesson. Then plot your reading speed on the graph by putting a small X on the line directly above the number of the lesson, across from the number of words per minute you read. As you mark your speed for each lesson, graph your progress by drawing a line to connect the X's.

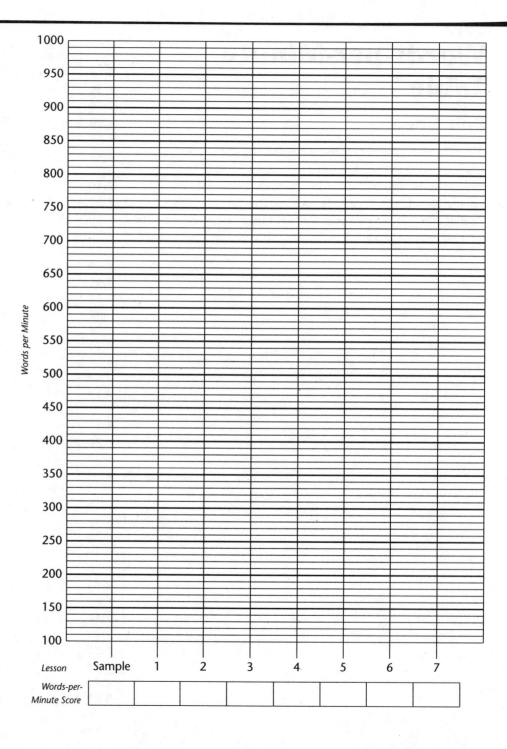

Lesson	Sample	1	2	3	4	5	6	7
Words-per-Minute Score								

Plotting Your Progress: Reading Comprehension

Unit One

Directions: Write your Reading Comprehension score for each lesson in the box under the number of the lesson. Then plot your score on the graph by putting a small X on the line directly above the number of the lesson and across from the score you earned. As you mark your score for each lesson, graph your progress by drawing a line to connect the X's.

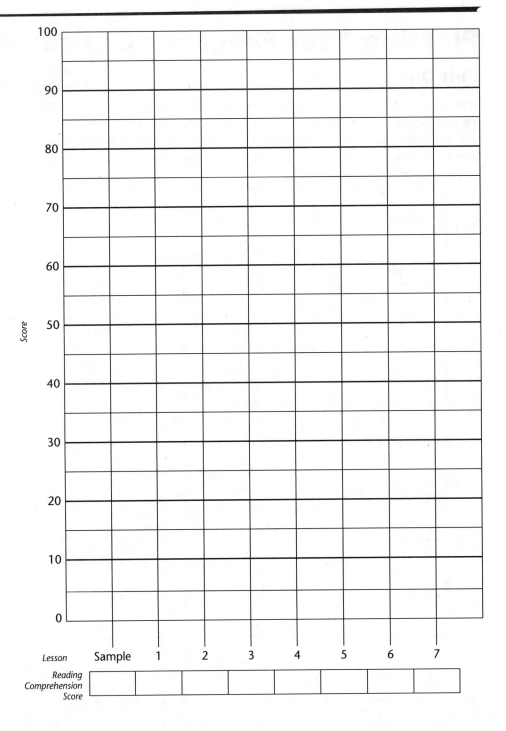

Lesson	Sample	1	2	3	4	5	6	7
Reading Comprehension Score								

Plotting Your Progress: Critical Thinking

Unit One

Directions: Work with your teacher to evaluate your responses to the Critical Thinking questions for each lesson. Then fill in the appropriate spaces in the chart below. For each lesson and each type of Critical Thinking question, do the following: Mark a minus sign (–) in the box to indicate areas in which you feel you could improve. Mark a plus sign (+) to indicate areas in which you feel you did well. Mark a minus-slash-plus sign (–/+) to indicate areas in which you had mixed success. Then write any comments you have about your performance, including ideas for improvement.

Lesson	Author's Approach	Summarizing and Paraphrasing	Critical Thinking
Sample			
1			
2			
3			
4			
5			
6			
7			

UNIT TWO

URI GELLER
Is He for Real?

Linda Cristal holds a spoon that Uri Geller (left) bent using psychokinesis powers.

Does Uri Geller belong in a book titled *Deceptions*? Geller and his supporters would surely say no. But skeptics, most notably James "The Amazing" Randi, believe Geller absolutely does belong here. Randi, who is a magician himself, claims that what Geller does is no more than the parlor tricks of a magician. Geller disputes that. He says he is not a magician; he is a psychic whose mental powers allow him to do the most extraordinary things.

2   Uri Geller thinks he may have gotten his powers through an encounter with a UFO. It happened, he says, when he was a small boy. One day he heard a terrific noise. Then he saw a burning ball. The ball emitted a ray which pierced him. From that day on, Geller says, he began to notice that he had some unusual powers. He could make a clock go faster by concentrating hard on it. (He did this in school so the class would end earlier.) Geller could also bend spoons at the dinner table using nothing but the power of his mind.

3   Geller slowly developed his powers as he grew into adulthood. He served in the Israeli army as a paratrooper. Later, he worked as a fashion model. In 1969, he began to show his powers to selected groups of people. Geller bent spoons and

made seemingly broken watches run again. He would also ask people to draw something on a piece of paper that he couldn't see. He would then read their minds and tell them what they had drawn. Some people found his act quite impressive. One day, he got his big break. He met Golda Meir, the Prime Minister of Israel. "At a party she did a drawing, and she did it in the toilet, and I read her mind," recalls Geller.

4   Later, Golda Meir was being interviewed on a national radio program. She was asked what she saw for the future of Israel. The Prime Minister replied, "Don't ask me. Ask Uri Geller." That, Geller acknowledged, was the biggest plug of his life. Soon people from all over were asking him to perform. In 1973, Geller appeared on British TV. He shocked the entire nation by breaking a steel fork just by stroking it. He even willed a broken watch to mend itself.

5   Uri Geller soon came under severe attack. Critics said that he had no special psychic powers; he was just a gifted magician. Geller fought back. In a series of closely-watched scientific experiments, he impressed many fair-minded people. "I was tested in laboratories all around the world," Geller said later. "No one can explain [the powers], but I was validated."

6   The most widely-known of these tests was conducted by the Stanford Research Institute. In one experiment, Geller was asked to determine the value of a single die which was placed in a closed metal box and shaken. He got the correct answer eight out of ten times. The odds against that are about a million to one. In another experiment, ten identical cans were arranged in a row. While Geller was out of the room, an object was placed underneath one of the cans. Geller was then asked to select the can which hid the object. He chose the correct can 12 times without error. The odds against that level of accuracy were estimated at one in a trillion.

7   Scientists Harold Puthoff and Russell Targ conducted the tests. They were impressed, but reluctant to jump to any conclusions. "We do not claim that [Geller] has psychic powers," they wrote. "We draw no sweeping conclusions as to the nature of these phenomena.... All we can say at this point is that further investigation is clearly warranted."

8   Other research teams have been impressed as well. At the University of London, Geller amazed physicists by making a Geiger counter register 500 times its normal count. At a U.S. Naval weapons center he caused an alloy,

Nitinol, to become deformed. At a university in Japan, before a watchful team of scientists, he erased a computer tape without touching it.

Magician James Randi, who received a MacArthur Foundation "genius grant," insists that Geller is nothing more than a skilled magician.

9   Still, Geller hasn't convinced his opponents. Says James Randi, "Everything that Mr. Geller does in his standard routine is straight out of the book of magic." Fooling people, even very smart people, is the art of a magician. Scientists, for instance, are not usually well versed in magic tricks. They don't understand how a good magician can seemingly defy the laws of nature. So they may not be the best people to run the tests.

10   Bending spoons, for example, is done by misdirection. One way or another, Randi claims, Geller gets people to look elsewhere while he bends the spoon with his fingers. "Broken" watches are often just clogged up. Almost anyone can get them started again by warming and shaking the watch. Keeping it running, Randi says, is a harder trick. But that is never tested during the short time Geller is on stage. "Please understand that I'm not putting him down as a performer," Randi says. "He's skilled, he's creative, but there's no evidence that it's supernatural."

11   Geller hasn't always performed very well. He seems to do best when he sets his own ground rules. Once he appeared on the *Tonight Show with Johnny Carson*, where he was supposed to bend a spoon and to make a watch stop keeping time. But Geller didn't do either of those things. In fact, he didn't even try. Some people hinted that Randi and Carson had switched spoons on him. (Critics contend that Geller likes to use his own spoons which he warms, or softens, before his act.)

12   Geller had his own explanation for his apparent failure. He explained that his power can't be turned on and off like a radio or a television. He admits that sometimes the spoon doesn't bend. "That happens," he says. "I have to be in the mood. It's a power or an energy that I have to trigger."

13   Still, Uri Geller does seem to do some pretty incredible things. In 1996, the London *Sunday Telegraph* reported that a long lost submarine had been found. Eight years earlier, a radio producer had asked Geller about the same submarine. The producer meant it as a joke. But Geller named a spot. It was found just yards away from where Geller said it was. "I don't know how he did it, or if it was just pure chance," said the producer, "but it was [right on]."

14   Who's right—Geller or Randi? Uri Geller has sued James Randi for libel and lost. Yet the larger issue is still open. Just how powerful is the human mind? Scientists are only now beginning to investigate that question. 🍃

If you have been timed while reading this article, enter your reading time below. Then turn to the Words-per-Minute Table on page 133 and look up your reading speed (words per minute). Enter your reading speed on the graph on page 134.

Reading Time: Lesson 8

_____ : _____
Minutes   Seconds

A Finding the Main Idea

One statement below expresses the main idea of the article. One statement is too general, or too broad. The other statement explains only part of the article; it is too narrow. Label the statements using the following key:

M—Main Idea   **B—Too Broad**   **N—Too Narrow**

_____   1. Uri Geller is known around the world for his incredible, almost supernatural powers.

_____   2. Uri Geller can do amazing tricks with his mind such as bending spoons and erasing computer files.

_____   3. Although psychic Uri Geller seems to have amazing mental abilities, many critics refuse to believe in him.

_____   Score 15 points for a correct M answer.

_____   Score 5 points for each correct B or N answer.

_____   **Total Score:** Finding the Main Idea

B Recalling Facts

How well do you remember the facts in the article? Put an X in the box next to the answer that correctly completes each statement about the article.

1. Uri Geller traces his amazing powers back to the day when he
    - ☐ a. was pierced by a ray from a burning ball.
    - ☐ b. was struck by lightning.
    - ☐ c. joined the Israeli army.

2. According to the article, Geller's psychic powers have been tested by
    - ☐ a. the FBI.
    - ☐ b. the Stanford Research Institute.
    - ☐ c. the government of Israel.

3. In an experiment at a U.S. weapons center, Geller
    - ☐ a. deformed an alloy using his mind only.
    - ☐ b. read the minds of the testers.
    - ☐ c. started a stopped watch.

4. One of Geller's most vocal critics is
    - ☐ a. scientist Harold Puthoff.
    - ☐ b. Prime Minister Golda Meir.
    - ☐ c. magician James Randi.

5. Critics believe that anyone can restart a stopped watch by
    - ☐ a. warming and shaking it.
    - ☐ b. concentrating on it.
    - ☐ c. placing it in an airtight, metal container.

Score 5 points for each correct answer.

_____   **Total Score:** Recalling Facts

C **Making Inferences**

When you combine your own experience and information from a text to draw a conclusion that is not directly stated in that text, you are making an inference. Below are five statements that may or may not be inferences based on information in the article. Label the statements using the following key:

C—Correct Inference   **F—Faulty Inference**

_____ 1. Only Americans are willing to take the time to test Uri Geller's amazing abilities.

_____ 2. Uri Geller believes that there is life in places in the universe other than Earth.

_____ 3. Uri Geller's main goal in life is to help others by using his amazing powers.

_____ 4. At one time, Uri Geller was famous in many countries.

_____ 5. If critics are correct when they say that Geller is a good magician, it follows that he cannot have unusual mental powers.

Score 5 points for each correct answer.

_____ **Total Score:** Making Inferences

D **Using Words Precisely**

Each numbered sentence below contains an underlined word or phrase from the article. Following the sentence are three definitions. One definition is closest to the meaning of the underlined word. One definition is opposite or nearly opposite. Label those two definitions using the following key. Do not label the remaining definition.

C—Closest   **O—Opposite or Nearly Opposite**

1. But <u>skeptics</u>, most notably James "The Amazing" Randi, believe Geller absolutely does belong here.

_____ a. trusting people

_____ b. people who doubt

_____ c. entertainers

2. Geller <u>disputes</u> that.

_____ a. agrees with

_____ b. tries

_____ c. argues against

3. "No one can explain [the powers], but I was <u>validated</u>."

_____ a. frightened

_____ b. found to be authentic

_____ c. uncovered as false

4. They were impressed, but <u>reluctant</u> to jump to any conclusions.

_____ a. unwilling

_____ b. eager

_____ c. proud

5. Critics <u>contend</u> that Geller likes to use his own spoons which he warms, or softens, before his act.

_____ a. predict

_____ b. deny

_____ c. maintain

_____ Score 3 points for each correct C answer.

_____ Score 2 points for each correct O answer.

_____ **Total Score:** Using Words Precisely

Enter the four total scores in the spaces below, and add them together to find your Reading Comprehension Score. Then record your score on the graph on page 135.

Score	Question Type	Lesson 8
_____	Finding the Main Idea	
_____	Recalling Facts	
_____	Making Inferences	
_____	Using Words Precisely	
_____	**Reading Comprehension Score**	

Author's Approach

Put an X in the box next to the correct answer.

1. What does the author mean by the statement "One day, he got his big break"?

☐ a. One day, Geller broke the news of his amazing abilities to his friends and family.

☐ b. One day, Geller broke one of his bones.

☐ c. One day, an incident happened that made Geller famous.

2. The main purpose of the first paragraph is to

☐ a. introduce the reader to both Geller and his critics

☐ b. entertain the reader with stories about Geller.

☐ c. persuade readers to believe in Geller.

3. Which of the following statements from the article best describes Geller's response to his critics?

☐ a. "Geller slowly developed his powers as he grew into adulthood."

☐ b. "Geller fought back. In a series of closely-watched scientific experiments, he impressed many fair-minded people."

☐ c. "…he was supposed to bend a spoon and to make a watch stop keeping time. But Geller didn't do either of those things."

CRITICAL THINKING

4. Choose the statement below that best describes the author's position in paragraph 14.

☐ a.   The fact that Uri Geller lost a libel suit against Randi proves that he has no psychic powers.

☐ b.   Uri Geller may or may not have psychic powers, but he makes us wonder about the powers of the human mind.

☐ c.   It has been proven that Uri Geller definitely has psychic powers.

_____ Number of correct answers

Record your personal assessment of your work on the Critical Thinking Chart on page 136.

Summarizing and Paraphrasing

Follow the directions provided for question 1. Put an X in the box next to the correct answer for question 2.

1. Look for the important ideas and events in paragraphs 11 and 12. Summarize those paragraphs in one or two sentences.

_____

_____

_____

2. Choose the sentence that correctly restates the following sentence from the article:

"He [Geller] seems to do best when he sets his own ground rules."

☐ a.   Geller does his best work when the rules are clear.

☐ b.   Geller works best when he has control over every part of his performance.

☐ c.   Geller's performances are most interesting when he defies the laws of nature.

_____ Number of correct answers

Record your personal assessment of your work on the Critical Thinking Chart on page 136.

Critical Thinking

Follow the directions provided for question 1. Put an X in the box next to the correct answer for the other questions.

1. For each statement below, write O if it expresses an opinion and write F if it expresses a fact.

_____ a.   Everyone in Great Britain was impressed with Geller's abilities to break a steel fork just by touching it.

_____ b.   Geller is nothing but a skilled magician and has no psychic abilities.

_____ c.   Geller got the correct answer eight out of ten times in one experiment run by the Stanford Research Institute.

2. From what the article told about Uri Geller, you can predict that

☐ a. the next time Geller appears on TV, he will perform his act perfectly.

☐ b. scientists will soon prove beyond a doubt that Geller does have supernatural powers.

☐ c. no matter what Uri Geller does, Randi will not believe that Geller has supernatural powers.

3. How is Uri Geller related to James Randi?

☐ a. They both say that they have supernatural powers.

☐ b. They are both from Israel.

☐ c. They are both entertainers.

4. What did you have to do to answer question 3?

☐ a. find an opinion (what someone thinks about something)

☐ b. find a cause (why something happened)

☐ c. find a comparison (how things are the same)

_____ Number of correct answers

Record your personal assessment of your work on the Critical Thinking Chart on page 136.

Personal Response

A question I would like answered by Uri Geller is

_____

_____

_____

_____

Self-Assessment

Before reading this article, I already knew

_____

_____

_____

_____

JANET COOKE
Disgraced Journalist

Jimmy is 8 years old and a third generation heroin addict...."

2 So began a shocking article in the *Washington Post*. The article ran on September 28, 1980. It told all about Jimmy, an African-American boy who lived with his mother and her boyfriend. Their home was in the worst section of Washington, D.C. In that home, according to the paper, the boyfriend had been giving Jimmy shots of heroin since he was five years old. The article told of "needle marks freckling the baby-smooth skin of [Jimmy's] thin brown arms." It even followed Jimmy through an injection. It described how "the needle [slid] into the boy's soft skin like a straw pushed into the center of a freshly baked cake."

3 *Post* readers were outraged. They flooded the paper with phone calls. Everyone knew there were scores of addicts in the city, but no one could bear to think of such a life for an eight-year-old child. People cringed at the heartbreaking details of the story. They could picture

This run-down neighborhood in Washington, D.C., is the kind of area in which Janet Cooke set her story about Jimmy, a fictional eight-year-old heroin addict.

Jimmy's "velvety brown eyes," his fancy running shoes bought with drug money, the look on his face as he got high and drifted off into the addict's "nod." People demanded that something be done to get Jimmy out of his nightmarish situation. The police, too, put pressure on the newspaper to reveal where Jimmy lived so they could rescue him from his plight.

4   The editors at the *Post* stood firm. They refused to give out any more information about Jimmy. They said they would support their reporter's decision to keep her sources confidential.

5   Privately, *Post* editors were pleased that the article had generated so much community concern. It was a measure of how compelling the story was. They were proud of the bright young reporter who had written the piece. The reporter's name was Janet Cooke. She was only 26 years old and had been working at the *Post* less than two years. But clearly she was headed for great things in the world of journalism.

6   Janet Cooke had come to the *Post* from the *Toledo Blade*. This young African-American reporter was hired in part because of her strong credentials. Her résumé showed that she had graduated with honors from Vassar College. She had studied at the Sorbonne University in Paris. She held a master's degree from the

University of Toledo. And she spoke French, Spanish, Portuguese, and Italian.

7   Another plus for Cooke was her personal style. When she spoke with editors at the *Post*, she was poised and charming. She impressed almost everyone who met her, including Ben Bradlee, the executive editor. One more element in her favor was the *Post's* desire to hire more minority reporters and more female reporters. Cooke was both. And finally there were Cooke's writing samples. As Ben Bradlee later said, Janet Cooke "could write like a dream."

8   Given all those factors, *Post* editors found it easy to hire her. And Cooke wasted no time settling in. During her first eight months at the paper, she produced 52 articles. She told a friend that she hoped to win a Pulitzer Prize in three years. Her immediate editor was struck by Cooke's eagerness to get ahead. She described Cooke as "consumed by blind and raw ambition, but talented."

9   With the story about "Jimmy's World," Cooke's dream of a Pulitzer Prize suddenly seemed within reach. Editors at the paper thought so highly of the piece that they entered it in that year's Pulitzer competition. It was the only article submitted by the *Post* in the category of local news reporting.

10   Not everyone was a fan of Janet Cooke's story. A fellow reporter named Courtland Milloy was skeptical. Milloy was an African-American reporter who had a good feel for the streets of Washington, D.C. In an attempt to verify the story, he asked to see where Jimmy lived. Cooke rode around the city with him, but couldn't find the right house.

Washington Post *editor Ben Bradlee*

Disturbed, Milloy went to the city editor. The editor thought Milloy was just jealous of Cooke's big story. None of the paper's white editors had any first-hand knowledge of the kind of world Cooke's story described. They had to trust her. Besides, the details Cooke included in her writing struck them as too authentic to question.

11   On April 13, 1981, the Pulitzer Prizes were announced. Janet Cooke's story about "Jimmy's World" was a winner. Ben Bradlee and his editors were thrilled. But their excitement didn't last long. Later that day, Bradlee got a call from an admissions officer at Vassar. It seemed the college had no record of Cooke ever receiving a diploma. In fact, records showed that she had spent just one year at Vassar. With a sinking feeling, Bradlee realized that no one at the *Post* had ever checked Cooke's credentials. They had all just assumed her résumé was truthful.

12   The bad news didn't end there. A few minutes later, Bradlee learned that some of the other items on Cooke's résumé looked suspicious. Back when she had worked at the *Toledo Blade*, she had never mentioned having a master's degree. She had not listed the Sorbonne among her credentials. And she had not claimed to speak five languages.

13   Bradlee and several of his editors met with Cooke. She burst into tears and admitted she had lied about having a Vassar degree. But everything else in her résumé, she said, was the truth. Bradlee decided to test that assertion. He started with her language training. Would she please say two words in Portuguese? She said she couldn't. He asked her to speak Italian. She couldn't. He began asking her questions in French. She had no idea what he was saying. Angrily, Bradlee told Cooke that she had 24 hours to prove the Jimmy story was true. Then he stormed out of the room.

14   One of the other editors suggested that Cooke show him where Jimmy lived. In her story, she had described his apartment down to the tiniest details. She had told of the brown shag rug, fake bamboo blinds, and eight-foot sofa. Cooke hadn't been able to show Courtland Milloy where Jimmy lived; could she show someone now? For half an hour, Cooke tried, but once again, she couldn't seem to locate the house.

15   At last, late that night, Janet Cooke confessed. There was no Jimmy; he did not exist. He was, she said, a "composite character." In other words, Cooke had made him up by combining elements of many people she had interviewed. Cooke admitted she had been wrong to pretend that Jimmy was real person. She said she had been praying she wouldn't win the Pulitzer Prize.

16   The *Post* allowed Cooke to resign. The next morning, Ben Bradlee called the Pulitzer committee to tell them the prize was being returned. The episode was a major embarrassment for the *Post*. Moreover, it spelled the end of Janet Cooke's journalistic career. Her next job was salesclerk in a department store.

If you have been timed while reading this article, enter your reading time below. Then turn to the Words-per-Minute Table on page 133 and look up your reading speed (words per minute). Enter your reading speed on the graph on page 134.

Reading Time: Lesson 9

_____ : _____
Minutes   Seconds

A Finding the Main Idea

One statement below expresses the main idea of the article. One statement is too general, or too broad. The other statement explains only part of the article; it is too narrow. Label the statements using the following key:

M—Main Idea   **B—Too Broad**   **N—Too Narrow**

_____ 1. Janet Cooke's foolish actions caused embarrassment for her employer and disaster for her career.

_____ 2. Though Janet Cooke claimed to have interviewed a young addict named Jimmy at home, she couldn't locate his house later.

_____ 3. Janet Cooke's award-winning article about an eight-year-old drug addict was both shocking and false, and it eventually cost her her job.

_____ Score 15 points for a correct M answer.

_____ Score 5 points for each correct B or N answer.

_____ **Total Score:** Finding the Main Idea

B Recalling Facts

How well do you remember the facts in the article? Put an X in the box next to the answer that correctly completes each statement about the article.

1. When they read Cooke's article about a young addict named Jimmy, readers
   ☐ a. requested that Cooke write more articles about Jimmy.
   ☐ b. demanded that something be done to help him.
   ☐ c. were so moved that they demanded that Cooke be given the Pulitzer Prize.

2. Janet Cooke's résumé claimed that she had graduated from
   ☐ a. Georgetown University.
   ☐ b. Stanford University.
   ☐ c. Vassar College.

3. Fellow reporter Courtland Milloy asked Cooke to show him where Jimmy lived because he wanted to
   ☐ a. verify Cooke's incredible story.
   ☐ b. help Jimmy overcome his addiction.
   ☐ c. write another story about Jimmy.

4. Finally, Janet Cooke confessed that Jimmy was
   ☐ a. just an actor pretending to be an addict.
   ☐ b. dead.
   ☐ c. a character she made up from other characters.

5. When *Post* editors found out that the article was a fraud, they
   ☐ a. tried to cover up the scandal.
   ☐ b. sent back the Pulitzer Prize.
   ☐ c. forgave Cooke for this understandable mistake.

Score 5 points for each correct answer.

_____ **Total Score:** Recalling Facts

C Making Inferences

When you combine your own experience and information from a text to draw a conclusion that is not directly stated in that text, you are making an inference. Below are five statements that may or may not be inferences based on information in the article. Label the statements using the following key:

C—Correct Inference   F—Faulty Inference

_____ 1. Plenty of applicants for the position of journalist had credentials similar to Janet Cooke's.

_____ 2. Without a doubt, there was a person exactly like Jimmy in Washington, D.C.

_____ 3. The printed word has the power to excite and interest readers.

_____ 4. If Janet Cooke's article hadn't won the Pulitzer Prize, the deception would never have been revealed.

_____ 5. The editors of the *Post* valued truth more than the Pulitzer Prize.

Score 5 points for each correct answer.

_____ **Total Score:** Making Inferences

D Using Words Precisely

Each numbered sentence below contains an underlined word or phrase from the article. Following the sentence are three definitions. One definition is closest to the meaning of the underlined word. One definition is opposite or nearly opposite. Label those two definitions using the following key. Do not label the remaining definition.

C—Closest   O—Opposite or Nearly Opposite

1. The police, too, put pressure on the newspaper to reveal where Jimmy lived so they could rescue him from his <u>plight</u>.

_____ a. difficult situation

_____ b. family

_____ c. fortunate condition

2. Privately, *Post* editors were pleased that the article had <u>generated</u> so much community concern.

_____ a. put an end to

_____ b. created

_____ c. highlighted

3. It was a measure of how <u>compelling</u> the story was.

_____ a. distasteful

_____ b. weak

_____ c. forceful and attention-getting

4. Her <u>immediate</u> editor was struck by Cooke's eagerness to get ahead.

_____ a. nearest

_____ b. most remote or farthest away

_____ c. fast-paced

5. Besides, the details Cooke included in her writing struck them as too <u>authentic</u> to question.

_____ a. complicated

_____ b. real or genuine

_____ c. fictional

_____ Score 3 points for each correct C answer.

_____ Score 2 points for each correct O answer.

_____ **Total Score:** Using Words Precisely

Enter the four total scores in the spaces below, and add them together to find your Reading Comprehension Score. Then record your score on the graph on page 135.

Score	Question Type	Lesson 9
_____	Finding the Main Idea	
_____	Recalling Facts	
_____	Making Inferences	
_____	Using Words Precisely	
_____	**Reading Comprehension Score**	

Author's Approach

Put an X in the box next to the correct answer.

1. The author uses the first sentence of the article to

☐ a. entertain the reader with the beginning of a heartwarming story.

☐ b. describe the qualities of life in a typical urban household.

☐ c. inform the reader about the way Janet Cooke's prize-winning article began.

2. What does the author mean by the statement "Another plus for Cooke was her personal style"?

☐ a. Cooke's way of speaking and writing made her a desirable employee at the *Post*.

☐ b. Cooke's way of speaking and acting was one more strike against her when she tried to get a job at the *Post*.

☐ c. Cooke was not only a good writer; she was also naturally skillful at arithmetic.

3. Judging from statements in the article "Janet Cooke: Disgraced Journalist," you can conclude that the author wants the reader to think that

☐ a. Janet Cooke purposely wrote "Jimmy's World" in order to embarrass the editors of the *Washington Post*.

☐ b. Because Janet Cooke wanted fame so badly, she made a terrible mistake.

☐ c. In reality, Janet Cooke did not care much for the children of the city of Washington, D.C.

_____ Number of correct answers

Record your personal assessment of your work on the Critical Thinking Chart on page 136.

Summarizing and Paraphrasing

Follow the directions provided for the these questions.

1. Complete the following one-sentence summary of the article using the lettered phrases from the phrase bank below. Write the letters on the lines.

> **Phrase Bank:**
> a. the editor of the *Post* sending back the Pulitzer Prize
> b. how Cooke's deception was discovered and dealt with
> c. a description of Cooke's article

The article about Janet Cooke begins with _____, goes on to explain _____, and ends with _____.

2. Reread paragraph 12 in the article. Below, write a summary of the paragraph in no more than 25 words.

_____

_____

_____

_____

Reread your summary and decide if the summary covers important parts of the paragraph. Next, decide how to shorten the summary to 15 words or less without leaving out any essential information. Write this summary below.

_____

_____

_____

_____ Number of correct answers

Record your personal assessment of your work on the Critical Thinking Chart on page 136.

Critical Thinking

Follow the directions provided for questions 1, 3, 4, and 5. Put an X in the box next to the correct answer for question 2.

1. For each statement below, write O if it expresses an opinion and write F if it expresses a fact.

_____ a. Janet Cooke wrote 52 articles during her first eight months as a journalist at the *Post*.

_____ b. Courtland Milloy was jealous of Janet Cooke's success.

_____ c. No one at the *Post* had ever checked Cooke's credentials before she won the Pulitzer Prize.

2. Based on the information in paragraph 16, you can predict that

☐ a. the Pulitzer committee will never award one of their prizes to anyone from the *Post* again.

☐ b. the *Post* will never take a chance on a young writer again.

☐ c. Janet Cooke will never write for the *Post* again.

3. Choose from the letters below to correctly complete the following statement. Write the letters on the lines.

In the article, _____ and _____ are different.

a. the home life of people who live in Paris

b. the home life of many of the white editors at the *Post*

c. the home life of poor African-American children in Washington, D.C.

4. Read paragraph 10. Then choose from the letters below to correctly complete the following statement. Write the letters on the lines.

According to paragraph 10, _____ happened because _____.

a. Courtland Milloy reported his doubts about the truthfulness of Cooke's article to the city editor

b. Courtland Milloy was an African-American reporter who knew Washington, D.C., well

c. Janet Cooke couldn't locate Jimmy's house

5. In which paragraph did you find your information or details to answer question 3?

_____

_____ Number of correct answers

Record your personal assessment of your work on the Critical Thinking Chart on page 136.

Personal Response

Would you recommend this article to other students? Explain.

_____

_____

_____

_____

_____

Self-Assessment

A word or phrase in the article that I do not understand is

_____

_____

_____

_____

CRITICAL THINKING

THE KING OF ROMANCE
(and Deception)

This 19th century Valentine card is titled "Faith and Love."

It was a boisterous scene. An excited crowd, mostly women, lined up at a courthouse in Phoenix, Arizona. They all hoped to get a seat in the small courtroom for the trial of Giovanni Vigliotto. Many, anticipating a long wait in line, brought along ice chests filled with food and drinks. Those who got seats refused to give them up during the 90-minute lunch break. None wanted to risk losing her seat. And none wanted to miss the latest installment in the romantic adventures of Vigliotto.

2   It was 1983. Vigliotto was on trial for bigamy and fraud. A bigamist is a person who has two or more spouses at the same time. But the 53-year-old defendant was no ordinary bigamist with a couple of wives. He was a world champion bigamist. In fact, his name is in the *Guinness Book of World Records*. In the space of 33 years, he married 105 women—and he never bothered to divorce any of them. Vigliotto romanced women from 26 states and 14 countries. Clearly, he was good at it. In fact, he once managed to marry four different women while sailing on one cruise ship.

3   Criminal charges were finally brought against Vigliotto by Patricia Ann Gardiner. She was wife number 105. She had married Vigliotto after an eight-day, whirlwind romance. He had impressed her with tales of his great wealth. And he seemed so nice. "He looked right into my face and eyes," Gardiner told the court. "I liked that honest trait." Vigliotto convinced her to sell her house in Arizona. The bride and groom then set off for California in two cars. Vigliotto drove a van filled with $36,000 worth of cash and valuables. Gardiner drove the other car with her pet poodle. By the time she reached a San Diego hotel, Vigliotto had vanished with all the loot. Gardiner had only her poodle to console her.

4   That was how Vigliotto operated—love 'em and leave 'em. Since he worked as a trader, he met many of his future wives at antique shows and flea markets. For the most part, he went after lonely, middle-aged women. Vigliotto would turn on the charm and, before long, these women would think they had met the man of their dreams. Often, they married within days or a couple of weeks. Vigliotto would smooth-talk them into turning over their assets to him. He would set a date to meet in another city. Then he would just vanish with the money. Naturally, many of his wives complained. But the police usually dismissed them by saying it was really a family matter and that they should get a good lawyer.

5   Vigliotto did not always have to marry to steal a woman's cash. One of the witnesses against him was Joan Bacarella of New Jersey. Bacarella had split from her husband, but she was not legally divorced. Still, Vigliotto swept her completely off her feet. Soon he drove off with $40,000 worth of merchandise from her clothing store. He never came back to the motel where Bacarella was waiting for him with her mother and three children. "I realized," she later said, "I had been victimized, and my prince [had] turned into a frog."

6   Of course, none of his wives liked being robbed blind or being made to look like fools. But by the time they realized Vigliotto was nothing but a con man, he was long gone. And he wasn't an easy man to track. Over his long career, he used more than 50 aliases. Even his own lawyer said that Vigliotto had used so many different names, "I'm not sure that even he remembers his real name."

7   One woman, however, refused to just let it go. Her name was Sharon Clark and she was wife number 104. She met Vigliotto in 1981 while she was managing an amusement park in Indiana. For a while, he helped her run the park and even helped it turn a profit. "He seemed a natural leader," Clark recalled. "He was

Romancer and bigamist Giovanni Vigliotto leaves a Phoenix courtroom.

fabulous with people... he talked to them, and they liked him."

8   A few weeks later, Clark and Vigliotto got married. They drove to Tennessee, where, as Clark said, they found "an old preacher in bib overalls who hadn't shaved in two or three days." The preacher put on a wrinkled shirt and a pair of pants and performed "a quickie marriage." Then Vigliotto did his thing. He packed up about $49,000 worth of Clark's antiques and told her he would meet her in Canada in a few days.

9   When Vigliotto failed to show up, Clark went hunting for him. For six months, she doggedly kept after him. She followed antique shows because she knew he would be trying to sell the stuff he had stolen from her. The trail took her from Indiana to Arkansas to Texas to Mississippi to Florida. All along the way there were signs of Giovanni," she told the court. "I kept coming up with my things that he had sold along the way."

10   At last, Clark saw his van in Panama City, Florida. She slashed his tires so he could not drive away. Then she called the police. Officers arrested Vigliotto. They sent him to Arizona to face charges for defrauding Patricia Gardiner.

11   At his trial, Gardiner, Bacarella, and Clark testified against him. Vigliotto was willing to plead guilty to bigamy. But he insisted he was innocent of the fraud charge. During the year he spent in jail before his trail, he drew up his list of 105

wives. It wasn't easy remembering all those names and years. But as he said, "I've had a lot of time to think." Vigliotto put on quite a show for the people who waited in line to watch the trial. He fired his state-appointed lawyer only to hire him back. He cried openly in court and once tried to storm out of the courtroom.

12   Vigliotto's claim of innocence didn't sway the jury of eight men and four women. They found him guilty of fraud as well as bigamy. It took them just 90 minutes to reach a verdict. Giovanni Vigliotto looked shocked when he heard the word "guilty." After all, he had always gotten his way before. Women always said yes to him. But this jury said a resounding no. 🍃

If you have been timed while reading this article, enter your reading time below. Then turn to the Words-per-Minute Table on page 133 and look up your reading speed (words per minute). Enter your reading speed on the graph on page 134.

Reading Time: Lesson 10

_____ : _____
Minutes   Seconds

A **Finding the Main Idea**

One statement below expresses the main idea of the article. One statement is too general, or too broad. The other statement explains only part of the article; it is too narrow. Label the statements using the following key:

M—Main Idea   **B—Too Broad**   **N—Too Narrow**

_____ 1. Giovanni Vigliotto married 105 times, targeting lonely middle-aged women with money who married him within a few days.

_____ 2. Champion bigamist Giovanni Vigliotto was finally tracked down and brought to justice by a few of his 105 wives.

_____ 3. The story of Giovanni Vigliotto teaches the importance of learning as much as you can about the person you are about to marry.

_____ Score 15 points for a correct M answer.

_____ Score 5 points for each correct B or N answer.

_____ **Total Score:** Finding the Main Idea

 B **Recalling Facts**

How well do you remember the facts in the article? Put an X in the box next to the answer that correctly completes each statement about the article.

1. A bigamist is a person who
   - ☐ a. tricks others to get their money.
   - ☐ b. exaggerates in order to get into the record books.
   - ☐ c. has two or more spouses at the same time.

2. According to the article, Vigliotto met many of his wives at
   - ☐ a. church.
   - ☐ b. flea markets and antique shows.
   - ☐ c. the funerals of their first husbands.

3. Usually, after Vigliotto got a woman's possessions, he would
   - ☐ a. divorce her right away.
   - ☐ b. sell them back to her at a high price.
   - ☐ c. vanish without a trace.

4. Sharon Clark finally caught up with Vigliotto in
   - ☐ a. Panama City, Florida.
   - ☐ b. Palm Beach, California.
   - ☐ c. San Antonio, Texas.

5. At his trial, Vigliotto pleaded guilty to bigamy and not guilty to
   - ☐ a. libel.
   - ☐ b. fraud.
   - ☐ c. kidnapping.

Score 5 points for each correct answer.

_____ **Total Score:** Recalling Facts

C | Making Inferences

When you combine your own experience and information from a text to draw a conclusion that is not directly stated in that text, you are making an inference. Below are five statements that may or may not be inferences based on information in the article. Label the statements using the following key:

C—Correct Inference   **F—Faulty Inference**

_____ 1. Today, computer records make it impossible for people to be married to more than one person at a time.

_____ 2. All marriages on cruise ships are announced to everyone on board.

_____ 3. Vigliotto made every effort to restrict his activities to one or two states.

_____ 4. At his trial, Vigliotto proved that he was sorry for the all trouble he had caused his wives.

_____ 5. It was rather easy for the jurors to decide that Vigliotto was guilty of fraud and bigamy.

Score 5 points for each correct answer.

_____ **Total Score:** Making Inferences

D | Using Words Precisely

Each numbered sentence below contains an underlined word or phrase from the article. Following the sentence are three definitions. One definition is closest to the meaning of the underlined word. One definition is opposite or nearly opposite. Label those two definitions using the following key. Do not label the remaining definition.

C—Closest   O—Opposite or Nearly Opposite

1. It was a <u>boisterous</u> scene.

_____ a. peaceful

_____ b. noisy and rowdy

_____ c. beautiful

2. She had married Vigliotto after an eight-day, <u>whirlwind</u> romance.

_____ a. secret

_____ b. slow-paced

_____ c. very fast

3. For six months, she <u>doggedly</u> kept after him.

_____ a. stubbornly

_____ b. angrily

_____ c. showing a lack of determination

4. They sent him to Arizona to face charges for <u>defrauding</u> Patricia Gardiner.

_____ a. dealing honestly with

_____ b. tricking

_____ c. marrying

5. But this jury said a <u>resounding</u> no.

_____ a. loud

_____ b. surprising

_____ c. quiet

_____ Score 3 points for each correct C answer.

_____ Score 2 points for each correct O answer.

_____ **Total Score:** Using Words Precisely

Enter the four total scores in the spaces below, and add them together to find your Reading Comprehension Score. Then record your score on the graph on page 135.

Score	Question Type	Lesson 10
_____	Finding the Main Idea	
_____	Recalling Facts	
_____	Making Inferences	
_____	Using Words Precisely	
_____	**Reading Comprehension Score**	

Author's Approach

Put an X in the box next to the correct answer.

1. The author uses the first sentence of the article to
   - ☐ a. inform the reader about the laws concerning bigamy.
   - ☐ b. describe the qualities of the Vigliotto trial.
   - ☐ c. compare the inside of courthouse and the outside of the courthouse.

2. What is the author's purpose in writing "Giovanni Vigliotto: The King of Romance (and Deception)"?
   - ☐ a. To persuade the reader to pass laws against bigamy
   - ☐ b. To describe a situation in which a deceiver was captured and put on trial for his crimes
   - ☐ c. To convey a mood of peace and friendliness

3. From the statements below, choose those that you believe the author would agree with.
   - ☐ a. The women whom Vigliotto fooled were not very bright or resourceful.
   - ☐ b. Vigliotto simply misunderstood the law and didn't deserve to go to jail.
   - ☐ c. Vigliotto was unusually skillful at making people like him.

4. What does the author imply by saying "The preacher put on a wrinkled shirt and a pair of pants and performed 'a quickie marriage'"?
   - ☐ a. The preacher was not really authorized to perform the ceremony.
   - ☐ b. The marriage ceremony was performed in a very informal way.
   - ☐ c. The marriage was illegal.

_____ Number of correct answers

Record your personal assessment of your work on the Critical Thinking Chart on page 136.

Summarizing and Paraphrasing

Follow the directions provided for question 1. Put an X in the box next to the correct answer for the other questions.

1. Reread paragraph 8 in the article. Below, write a summary of the paragraph in no more than 25 words.

_____

_____

_____

Reread your summary and decide whether it covers the important ideas in the paragraph. Next, try to shorten the summary to 15 words or less without leaving out any essential information. Write this summary below.

_____

_____

_____

2. Read the statement about the article below. Then read the paraphrase of that statement. Choose the reason that best tells why the paraphrase does not say the same thing as the statement.

Statement: Usually, Vigliotto quickly talked each new wife into turning over all her assets to him, and then he disappeared.

Paraphrase: Vigliotto usually disappeared soon after each marriage, never to be seen again.

☐ a. Paraphrase says too much.

☐ b. Paraphrase doesn't say enough.

☐ c. Paraphrase doesn't agree with the statement about the article.

3. Choose the sentence that correctly restates the following sentence from the article:

"By the time they realized Vigliotto was nothing but a con man, he was long gone."

☐ a. Vigliotto disappeared before his victims could catch on to his tricks.

☐ b. Vigliotto was untrustworthy and devious.

☐ c. Vigliotto's victims were slow to understand how he had cheated them.

_____ Number of correct answers

Record your personal assessment of your work on the Critical Thinking Chart on page 136.

Critical Thinking

Put an X in the box next to the correct answer for questions 1, 3, and 4. Follow the directions provided for the other question.

1. Which of the following statements from the article is an opinion rather than a fact?

☐ a. "Vigliotto put on quite a show for the people who waited in line to watch the trial."

☐ b. "Criminal charges were finally brought against Vigliotto by Patricia Ann Gardner."

☐ c. "He never came back to the motel where Bacarella was waiting for him with her mother and three children."

2. Choose from the letters below to correctly complete the following statement. Write the letters on the lines.

According to the article, _____ and _____ are different.

a. the jury's judgment of Vigliotto

b. the judge's opinion of Vigliotto

c. many women's first responses to Vigliotto

3. What was the effect of Sharon Clark's slashing of Vigliotto's tires after she found him?

☐ a. Clark was arrested for destroying private property.

☐ b. Clark regretted that she had hurt Vigliotto's feelings.

☐ c. Vigliotto couldn't drive away before the police arrived.

4. What did you have to do to answer question 3?

☐ a. find an opinion (what someone thinks about something)

☐ b. find an effect (something that happened)

☐ c. find a definition (what something means)

_____ Number of correct answers

Record your personal assessment of your work on the Critical Thinking Chart on page 136.

Personal Response

I can't believe

_____

_____

_____

_____

Self-Assessment

The part I found most difficult about the article was

_____

_____

_____

I found this difficult because

_____

_____

_____

_____

CRITICAL THINKING

ALDRICH AMES
Traitor

Aldrich Ames, the highest-ranking CIA employee ever caught spying, leaves court after pleading guilty to espionage and tax evasion.

It came to a sudden end on February 21, 1994. Aldrich Ames left his home that morning, telling his wife he would be back shortly. He climbed into his wine-red XJ6 Jaguar and headed for CIA headquarters. But he didn't get very far. At a stop sign a few blocks from his house, Ames ran into an FBI roadblock. Several cars with red lights flashing surrounded him. America's most destructive traitor was under arrest.

2   The arrest of Aldrich Ames had been a long time coming. For 10 years he had betrayed his own country—the United States. Ames worked for the federal government's Central Intelligence Agency. The CIA spies on the country's enemies. At the same time, it tries to prevent these enemies from spying on us. People who work for the CIA often have access to America's most closely held secrets.

3   Ames sold out the United States to the former Soviet Union. He did it for the money—lots of money. Starting in 1985, the Soviets paid Ames $4.6 million for his treason. In return, Ames gave them what they wanted. He told them about America's top secret plans. No American had ever given an enemy so much. Ames

also betrayed his fellow CIA workers. The CIA had recruited some Soviets to work as spies for the United States. Ames gave their names to the Soviets, who moved quickly to arrest them. At least 10 of them were then tried, found guilty, and executed. About two dozen more were thrown into Soviet prisons.

4   Ironically, Aldrich Ames himself had never been a good spy. He had done spy work for a while but, although he was bright, his bosses gave him a series of dismal reports. He didn't win any points, for example, when he once left a safe open. The safe held many secrets as well as the combinations to other safes. Ames was also a heavy drinker. Once, while on duty in Italy, the police found him passed out drunk in a street gutter. Surprisingly, he was not fired. Instead, the CIA moved him to a desk job. He was put in charge of Soviet counterintelligence. Imagine, Ames was given the job of trying to stop the Soviets from spying on us!

5   Everyone now agrees that Ames should have been caught sooner. CIA officials knew he had problems. But for years they just looked the other way. They couldn't believe that one of their own would turn on them. But Ames did. His treason began on June 13, 1985. On that day, he took several plastic bags crammed with secrets and gave them to a Soviet agent named Chuvakhin. Never in U.S. history have so many classified files been given away in one day. And Ames didn't stop there. Over the next 12 months, he met with the Soviet agent at least 14 more times to leak secrets.

6   During that time, CIA agents working in the Soviet Union began to vanish. More and more were picked up, arrested, and shot. Ames had secretly given their names to the Soviets but at the time no one knew that. Americans couldn't figure out how the Soviets were uncovering the spies. Had the spies all made some mistake and gotten caught? Had the Soviets somehow tapped CIA phones? Had the Soviets broken a CIA code? Or did the enemy have a "mole"—a spy— inside the CIA? No one knew. But clearly something was wrong. The odds were against the CIA losing that many spies that fast without something being rotten.

7   Meanwhile, Aldrich Ames seemed to have plenty of money. His salary when he started working for the CIA was only about $50,000. Yet he was now driving an expensive Jaguar. He purchased an opulent house for $540,000 and paid for it with cash. (Most people, of course, need to get a loan from a bank to buy a house.) Ames bought rare paintings and pricey jewelry. He even opened up a Swiss bank account. In the past, he had worn rather

Aldrich Ames's home in Arlington, Virginia

shabby clothes but now he sported the latest fashions. Still, no one at the CIA seemed to notice or care.

8   Ames, who was divorced, remarried in 1985. His new wife was from Colombia. Her name was Maria del Rosario Casa. When Rosario found out what Ames was doing, she joined him. The two became partners in crime. She turned out to be just as greedy as he was. In fact, she might have been the stronger of the two. A former friend later said, "Rosario was the dominant figure. She led the way and [Ames] went along."

9   The CIA did not want to face the possibility that they might have a mole. However, none of their other ideas checked out. So, eventually, CIA officials had to look inside their own organization. Who could be selling secrets to the enemy? They started with a long list of suspects. They looked at anyone who had access to top secrets. It took time, but slowly they crossed off most of the names. The name of Aldrich Ames remained on the ever-dwindling list of suspects.

10   By 1990, CIA agents began to wonder how Ames could live so well on his pay. When they checked his bank records, one agent noticed that Ames had made a series of large deposits in 1985 and 1986. Soon, Ames was a prime suspect. In 1991, the FBI joined in the hunt. This was the first time the CIA and the FBI formed a joint mole-hunt team. Team agents questioned Ames. His answers were vague and

evasive. To nail him, the team needed proof that would hold up in court.

11   Secretly, FBI agents staked out the Ames house. Disguised as lawn workers and tree trimmers, they watched and waited. They bugged Ames's house and his car. They tapped his phones. They put a video camera in a tree across the street. The agents even combed through the trash. But week after week, nothing happened. They were sure they had the right man, but they couldn't prove it.

12   Then one evening, their efforts paid off. Under the cover of darkness, the agents rolled slowly down the street in a van with its headlights off. They snatched a full trash can from Ames's yard and replaced it with an identical, but empty, trash can. Returning to the van, the agents rifled through the garbage. They discovered a torn note arranging a secret meeting with a Soviet agent. Finally the agents were certain they had the right man. Ames was the mole.

13   The agents secured a search warrant, and waited until Ames and Rosario went out of town for a trip. The agents then entered the Ames house and began to look around. One agent downloaded all the files Ames had in his computer. Amazingly, Ames had kept a complete record of his treachery on his home computer. It was all there—the drop sites, the signals, the messages.

14   Still, the FBI wanted to catch Ames in the act, so they waited. Meanwhile,

Aldrich Ames continued to work for the CIA. Every day, he pulled into the parking lot in his fancy Jaguar. He went on regularly scheduled business trips. He even went to Moscow on CIA business, coming back $125,000 richer.

15   At last, the agents were tired of waiting. They didn't want to risk losing their man. After all, he might go to Moscow and never return. The order was given: "Bring him in." At the same time that Ames ran into the roadblock, other agents moved in on Rosario. Both were put on trial and found guilty. Rosario was sentenced to five years in prison. On April 28, 1994, Aldrich Ames was sentenced to life in prison with no hope for parole. He had done enough damage for one lifetime. 🍃

If you have been timed while reading this article, enter your reading time below. Then turn to the Words-per-Minute Table on page 133 and look up your reading speed (words per minute). Enter your reading speed on the graph on page 134.

Reading Time: **Lesson 11**

_____ : _____
Minutes   Seconds

Finding the Main Idea

One statement below expresses the main idea of the article. One statement is too general, or too broad. The other statement explains only part of the article; it is too narrow. Label the statements using the following key:

M—Main Idea   **B—Too Broad**   **N—Too Narrow**

_____ 1. For 10 years, Aldrich Ames leaked CIA information to America's enemies, but he was eventually captured and imprisoned for his treason.

_____ 2. With the money he made from selling U.S. government secrets to the Soviet Union, Aldrich Ames was able to go an a 10-year shopping spree.

_____ 3. Certainly Aldrich Ames is one of the most infamous traitors in the history of the United States.

_____ Score 15 points for a correct M answer.

_____ Score 5 points for each correct B or N answer.

_____ **Total Score:** Finding the Main Idea

 Recalling Facts

How well do you remember the facts in the article? Put an X in the box next to the answer that correctly completes each statement about the article.

1. For Ames's secrets, the Soviet Union paid about
   ☐ a. $1.5 million.
   ☐ b. $4.6 million.
   ☐ c. $124 million.

2. CIA stands for
   ☐ a. Central Intelligence of America.
   ☐ b. Central Information Agency.
   ☐ c. Central Intelligence Agency.

3. Ames became a prime suspect when CIA agents noticed that
   ☐ a. he was always late to work.
   ☐ b. unfamiliar people were coming to his house regularly and leaving with briefcases filled with papers.
   ☐ c. he was able to buy extremely expensive things that he couldn't afford on his pay.

4. Agents knew they had the right man when they looked though Ames's garbage and found
   ☐ a. a receipt for a deposit in a Swiss bank account.
   ☐ b. a note about a meeting with a Soviet agent.
   ☐ c. a note explaining how to crack a secret CIA code.

5. The scene of Ames's capture was
   ☐ a. his office at the CIA.
   ☐ b. the airport just before Ames was about to leave for Moscow.
   ☐ c. a roadblock set up near Ames's house.

Score 5 points for each correct answer.

_____ **Total Score:** Recalling Facts

C Making Inferences

When you combine your own experience and information from a text to draw a conclusion that is not directly stated in that text, you are making an inference. Below are five statements that may or may not be inferences based on information in the article. Label the statements using the following key:

C—Correct Inference   F—Faulty Inference

_____ 1. Only CIA employees with perfect records could be put in charge of important projects.

_____ 2. When CIA employees left work for the day, no one searched what they were taking out.

_____ 3. When they fear that a mole is at work, CIA agents quickly arrest any possible suspects.

_____ 4. American citizens' bank records are available to the CIA.

_____ 5. The FBI is so important that its agents don't need a search warrant to search a private citizen's home.

Score 5 points for each correct answer.

_____ **Total Score:** Making Inferences

D Using Words Precisely

Each numbered sentence below contains an underlined word or phrase from the article. Following the sentence are three definitions. One definition is closest to the meaning of the underlined word. One definition is opposite or nearly opposite. Label those two definitions using the following key. Do not label the remaining definition.

C—Closest   O—Opposite or Nearly Opposite

1. He had done spy work for a while but, although he was bright, his bosses gave him a series of dismal reports.

_____ a. dreadful

_____ b. interesting

_____ c. glowing

2. Never in U.S. history have so many classified files been given away in one day.

_____ a. available to everyone

_____ b. restricted to a few people

_____ c. personal

3. He purchased an opulent house for $540,000 and paid for it with cash.

_____ a. brick

_____ b. showy

_____ c. simple

4. His answers were <u>vague</u> and evasive.

_____ a. exact

_____ b. historic

_____ c. unclear

5. His answers were vague and <u>evasive</u>.

_____ a. expensive

_____ b. intended to cover up or conceal

_____ c. direct and to-the-point

_____ Score 3 points for each correct C answer.

_____ Score 2 points for each correct O answer.

_____ **Total Score:** Using Words Precisely

Enter the four total scores in the spaces below, and add them together to find your Reading Comprehension Score. Then record your score on the graph on page 135.

Score	Question Type	Lesson 11
_____	Finding the Main Idea	
_____	Recalling Facts	
_____	Making Inferences	
_____	Using Words Precisely	
_____	**Reading Comprehension Score**	

Author's Approach

Put an X in the box next to the correct answer.

1. What does the author mean by the statement in the first paragraph "It came to a sudden end on February 21, 1994"?
   - ☐ a. On that date, the CIA discovered that Aldrich Ames was a spy.
   - ☐ b. FBI and CIA interest in Aldrich Ames ended on that date.
   - ☐ c. On that date, Aldrich Ames's career as a spy ended.

2. From the statement from the article "He purchased an opulent house and paid for it with cash," you can conclude that the author wants the reader to think that
   - ☐ a. Ames boldly showed off his wealth, unworried about being caught.
   - ☐ b. Ames was an excellent saver who could afford an expensive home on a small salary.
   - ☐ c. Although Ames was selling CIA secrets, he was also a good, tax-paying homeowner.

3. How is the author's purpose for writing the article expressed in paragraph 3?
   - ☐ a. The author explains that some Soviets were working as spies for America.
   - ☐ b. The author explains that Ames turned traitor in order to get rich.
   - ☐ c. The author describes the fate of spies that Aldrich identified.

4. The author probably wrote this article in order to
   - ☐ a. entertain the reader with a humorous story.
   - ☐ b. encourage the reader to stay informed about current events.
   - ☐ c. reveal the details about an important event.

_____ Number of correct answers

Record your personal assessment of your work on the Critical Thinking Chart on page 136.

Summarizing and Paraphrasing

Follow the directions provided for question 1. Put an X in the box next to the correct answer for the other questions.

1. Look for the important ideas and events in paragraphs 7 and 8. Summarize those paragraphs in one or two sentences.

    _____

    _____

    _____

2. Read the statement about the article below. Then read the paraphrase of that statement. Choose the reason that best tells why the paraphrase does not say the same thing as the statement.

    Statement: This was the first time the CIA and the FBI had worked as a team to find a spy.

    Paraphrase: Until this case, the CIA and the FBI refused to cooperate with each other on any spy hunt.

    ☐ a.   Paraphrase says too much.

    ☐ b.   Paraphrase doesn't say enough.

    ☐ c.   Paraphrase doesn't agree with the statement about the article.

3. Choose the sentence that correctly restates the following sentence from the article:

    "To nail him, the team needed proof that would hold up in court."

    ☐ a.   To be sure that Ames would be convicted, the team needed proof that the court would accept.

    ☐ b.   To arrest Ames, the team needed new proof against him.

    ☐ c.   To be sure that Ames was really the mole, the team needed some proof.

_____ Number of correct answers

Record your personal assessment of your work on the Critical Thinking Chart on page 136.

Critical Thinking

Put an X in the box next to the correct answer for questions 1, 3, 4, and 5. Follow the directions provided for the other question.

1. Considering what the article told about Aldrich Ames's spy activities, you can predict that

    ☐ a.   the CIA now has more trust in its employees than it did before the Ames incident.

    ☐ b.   the CIA has worked to make it harder for employees to communicate secrets to other countries.

    ☐ c.   Ames will most likely be released from prison soon.

2. Choose from the letters below to correctly complete the following statement. Write the letters on the lines.

    On the positive side, _____, but on the negative side _____.

    a.   Rosaria found out about Ames's illegal activities

    b.   the CIA and FBI investigation took years, during which Ames was communicating government secrets

    c.   Ames was finally captured

3. What was the effect of Ames's treachery?

    ☐ a.   Spies for the United States were executed by the Soviets.

    ☐ b.   The Soviets learned for the first time that the United States didn't trust them.

    ☐ c.   Soviet spies were able to live freely in the United States.

4. How is the CIA related to the FBI?

☐ a. The CIA always works together with the FBI in solving crimes.

☐ b. They are both government organizations that investigate mysteries.

☐ c. Agents for both organizations act very quickly to stop crime.

5. Which paragraphs from the article provide evidence that supports your answer to question 3?

_____

_____ Number of correct answers

Record your personal assessment of your work on the Critical Thinking Chart on page 136.

Self-Assessment

A word or phrase in the article that I do not understand is

_____

_____

_____

_____

Personal Response

How do you think Rosario felt when she found out that her husband was working as a spy against the United States?

_____

_____

_____

ROSIE RUIZ
Marathon Fraud

It was the greatest upset in the 84-year history of the Boston Marathon. On April 21, 1980, Rosie Ruiz came out of nowhere to win the women's division. Her time was a record two hours, 31 minutes, and 56 seconds. Only two women had ever run a faster marathon. Incredibly, Ruiz had competed in just one other marathon. That one was in New York City. Yet Ruiz won the Boston race and she won it with style. Although she stumbled across the finish line, Ruiz was hardly sweating. Given the day's heat, that was pretty remarkable.

2   The Boston Marathon is America's oldest marathon. It starts in the small town of Hopkinton, Massachusetts. The runners—both men and women—then race 26 miles, 385 yards to downtown Boston. It's a rough and challenging race. There are lots of hills, the most notable being Heartbreak Hill. Every year many of the best runners in the world compete in the Boston Marathon.

3   In the early days of the race, women were not allowed to run. But by the 1970s, they were an accepted and welcomed part

Rosie Ruiz receives the laurel wreath for winning the Women's Division in the 1980 Boston Marathon. She was later stripped of her award when it was learned she hadn't run the entire distance.

of the race. Even though the top men run faster than the top women, the women's division is always as hotly contested as the men's. In 1980, Patti Lyons was the pre-race favorite. Jacqueline Gareau, Ellison Goodall, and Gillian Adams also figured to run well. No one gave Rosie Ruiz any thought at all.

4   The 1980 race had a large field—5,364 runners. The male leader, of course, was easy to notice. He was the first one coming down the road behind a fleet of Boston police motorcycles. The top woman, however, was a little harder to spot. She was often buried in a sea of male runners. Still, she could be identified because her race number began with the letter W. Besides, the attentive fans lining the course kept a sharp lookout for "the first woman."

5   Ellison Goodall started out on top. She heard shouts from the fans informing her that she was in the lead. That ended at the eight-mile mark. Jacqueline Gareau, with her powerful stride, shot past Goodall. A little while later Patti Lyons went by, too. At the 16-mile mark, Goodall heard a race photographer shout to her, "Number 22 [Gareau] is leading. Number 1 [Lyons] is second. You're third."

6   Now running in great pain, Goodall struggled just to get to the finish line. In the last six miles, three more women runners passed her. Goodall reached the finish line in a little over two hours and 42 minutes. Turning to one official, she said, "I guess sixth isn't so bad my first time out."

7   "But you were seventh," answered the official.

8   Goodall had never seen a sixth woman passing her, but she figured one must have. And that woman was on the winner's stand—with a medal around her neck and a laurel wreath on her head. Rosie Ruiz was wearing Number W50. Naturally, the sports reporters were showering her with questions. They all wanted to know more about this new racing superstar.

9   What Ruiz said made her feat even more astonishing. She had been running only a year and a half. Most top runners belong to a running club, but Ruiz didn't. She said that she had run track in high school and college, where her best time for the mile had been five minutes and 30 seconds. Somehow, she had improved a lot since then. Her average in the Boston Marathon was just five minutes and 46 seconds per mile. That meant she had maintained close to her top speed for over two and a half hours.

10   Another puzzling aspect to Ruiz's performance was her low profile throughout most of the race. No one saw her until the last few hundred yards. Goodall never saw Ruiz pass her, and neither did Gareau or Lyons. "People were saying I was [the] second woman at the fire station at 17 miles," recalled Lyons.

Wearing her winner's medal, Rosie Ruiz insists that she didn't cheat in order to win the 1980 Boston Marathon.

"And no woman could have passed me from then on without my seeing her."

11   As it turned out, there was a good reason why Rosie Ruiz had seemed so invisible. She hadn't run the entire distance of 26 miles, 385 yards. Her total mileage was more like 385 yards. Race officials later examined more than 10,000 photos of the race. Ruiz wasn't in any of them. Word circulated that while the rest of the field had been running, Ruiz had taken the subway. Witnesses later said they saw her climbing up the Kenmore Square subway steps. She had mingled a bit with the fans before stepping off the curb and into the race. She was later suspected of taking the subway in her New York City Marathon win, as well.

12   A few people smelled something fishy from the start. Bill Rodgers, the winner of the men's division, said, "I don't believe it. I don't believe that woman had run a marathon. She wasn't tired enough."

13   Doctor Yale Markle, a race official, examined some of the runners. After looking at Ruiz's feet, legs, ankles, and shoes, he said, "She definitely didn't run the whole race."

14   Rosie Ruiz, however, tearfully maintained her innocence. "I ran the race," she pleaded. "I don't know how to explain what I did. I just got up this morning with a lot of energy."

15   But Ruiz's story simply wasn't believable. For instance, she didn't understand racing terms such as "split" times. When asked about the course, all she could remember was that it was beautiful with "lots of houses and churches." When asked why none of the other women saw her, Ruiz said, "Since it was only my second race, I'm not familiar with watching out for where everybody is." Also, there was the problem with her pulse rate. Ruiz had a pulse rate of 76. That's healthy enough—for an office worker. Most world class marathon runners have pulse rates in the low 50s.

16   It took race officials eight days to check all the photos and interview witnesses. Then they made their decision. They stripped Rosie Ruiz of her title and gave it to Jacqueline Gareau, the rightful winner. When asked to return her medal, Ruiz refused. So officials had a new one made for Gareau. Kevin White, the mayor of Boston, presented the medal to Gareau at the finish line to the loud cheers of marathon fans everywhere.

17   Since then, Rosie Ruiz has faded into obscurity. But she is not totally forgotten in Boston. Cornwall's is a pub near the marathon finish line. On race day, the owner hangs out a white banner. It reads: "Rosie Ruiz Started Here!" 🍂

If you have been timed while reading this article, enter your reading time below. Then turn to the Words-per-Minute Table on page 133 and look up your reading speed (words per minute). Enter your reading speed on the graph on page 134.

Reading Time: Lesson 12

_____ : _____
Minutes   *Seconds*

A | Finding the Main Idea

One statement below expresses the main idea of the article. One statement is too general, or too broad. The other statement explains only part of the article; it is too narrow. Label the statements using the following key:

M—Main Idea   **B—Too Broad**   **N—Too Narrow**

_____ 1. No one in the history of the Boston Marathon has ever fooled race officials as skillfully as Rosie Ruiz.

_____ 2. Newcomer Rosie Ruiz won the 1980 Boston Marathon, but it was later determined that she hadn't run the entire race, so her medal was taken back.

_____ 3. Rosie Ruiz won the 1980 Boston Marathon, America's oldest marathon, with its field of 5,364 runners, both male and female.

_____ Score 15 points for a correct M answer.

_____ Score 5 points for each correct B or N answer.

_____ **Total Score:** Finding the Main Idea

B | Recalling Facts

How well do you remember the facts in the article? Put an X in the box next to the answer that correctly completes each statement about the article.

1. Rosie Ruiz had run in only one other race, in
   - ☐ a. New York City.
   - ☐ b. San Francisco.
   - ☐ c. Paris, France.

2. The length of the Boston Marathon is
   - ☐ a. 25 miles exactly.
   - ☐ b. 26 miles, 385 yards.
   - ☐ c. 21 miles, 385 yards.

3. In the more than 10,000 photos of the race, Rosie Ruiz
   - ☐ a. is near the back of the field of runners.
   - ☐ b. is leading all the way.
   - ☐ c. does not appear.

4. Winning runner Bill Rodgers doubted that Ruiz had run the whole race because
   - ☐ a. he hadn't seen her at the starting line.
   - ☐ b. he didn't think she looked tired enough.
   - ☐ c. she didn't know what a "split" time is.

5. When race officials asked Ruiz to return her medal, she
   - ☐ a. gave it back angrily.
   - ☐ b. refused to give it back.
   - ☐ c. finally admitted that she had cheated.

Score 5 points for each correct answer.

_____ **Total Score:** Recalling Facts

C | Making Inferences

When you combine your own experience and information from a text to draw a conclusion that is not directly stated in that text, you are making an inference. Below are five statements that may or may not be inferences based on information in the article. Label the statements using the following key:

C—Correct Inference   **F—Faulty Inference**

_____ 1. Many people, not just one photographer, took photos of the Boston Marathon.

_____ 2. It is common for runners in a marathon to run their top speed the entire distance.

_____ 3. Regular long-distance running usually lowers the runner's pulse rate.

_____ 4. At the Boston Marathon, the fans stand well back from path that the runners take.

_____ 5. The only place where marathon fans stand to view the race is the finish line.

Score 5 points for each correct answer.

_____ **Total Score:** Making Inferences

D | Using Words Precisely

Each numbered sentence below contains an underlined word or phrase from the article. Following the sentence are three definitions. One definition is closest to the meaning of the underlined word. One definition is opposite or nearly opposite. Label those two definitions using the following key. Do not label the remaining definition.

C—Closest   **O—Opposite or Nearly Opposite**

1. There are lots of hills, the most <u>notable</u> being Heartbreak Hill.

_____ a. difficult

_____ b. worthy of special attention

_____ c. common

2. Besides, the <u>attentive</u> fans lining the course kept a sharp lookout for "the first woman."

_____ a. alert

_____ b. closely-packed

_____ c. careless

3. What Ruiz said made her <u>feat</u> even more astonishing.

_____ a. an accomplishment that takes skill and courage

_____ b. an everyday, common activity

_____ c. lie

4. She had <u>mingled</u> a bit with the fans before stepping off the curb and into the race.

_____ a. separated from

_____ b. joked

_____ c. joined

5. Since then, Rosie Ruiz has faded into <u>obscurity</u>.

_____ a. dishonor

_____ b. fame

_____ c. the state of being unknown

_____ Score 3 points for each correct C answer.

_____ Score 2 points for each correct O answer.

_____ **Total Score:** Using Words Precisely

Enter the four total scores in the spaces below, and add them together to find your Reading Comprehension Score. Then record your score on the graph on page 135.

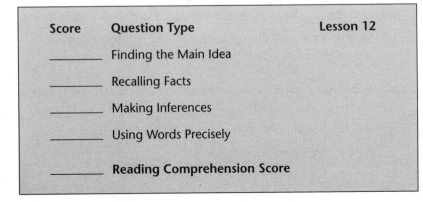

Score	Question Type	Lesson 12
_____	Finding the Main Idea	
_____	Recalling Facts	
_____	Making Inferences	
_____	Using Words Precisely	
_____	**Reading Comprehension Score**	

Author's Approach

Put an X in the box next to the correct answer.

1. The main purpose of the first paragraph is to

☐ a. To encourage readers to run in the Boston Marathon

☐ b. To describe the route of the Boston Marathon

☐ c. To describe an especially unusual moment in the 1980 Boston Marathon

2. Judging from the statement in the article "A few people smelled something fishy from the start," you can conclude that the author wants the reader to think that

☐ a. Certain people were alert enough not to be deceived.

☐ b. The people who didn't believe Ruiz's story were foolish.

☐ c. Some people refuse to believe anything good about strangers.

3. Choose the statement below that is the weakest argument for believing that Ruiz had really won the race.

☐ a. She had been a good runner in high school.

☐ b. She was fit and healthy.

☐ c. She cried in frustration when no one believed her story.

4. In this article, "Another puzzling aspect to Ruiz's performance was her low profile throughout most of the race" means

☐ a. no one could understand how Ruiz could look so calm throughout the race.

☐ b. it was surprising that no one had noticed Ruiz among the leading runners until the end of the race.

☐ c. it didn't make sense that the leading runners ignored Ruiz throughout the race.

_____ Number of correct answers

Record your personal assessment of your work on the Critical Thinking Chart on page 136.

CRITICAL THINKING

Summarizing and Paraphrasing

Follow the directions provided for question 1. Put an X in the box next to the correct answer for the other questions.

1. Complete the following one-sentence summary of the article using the lettered phrases from the phrase bank below. Write the letters on the lines.

Phrase Bank:
   a. the reaction of the officials to Ruiz's win
   b. the awarding of the medal to Jacqueline Gareau
   c. a description of the race

The article about Rosie Ruiz begins with _____, goes on to explain _____, and ends with _____.

2. Below are summaries of the article. Choose the summary that says all the most important things about the article but in the fewest words.

☐ a. Rosie Ruiz's medal was taken away after it was discovered that she did not run the entire race.

☐ b. The 1980 Boston Marathon, a 26-mile race that begins in Hopkinton, Massachusetts, and ends in Boston, was the scene of a fraud committed by Rosie Ruiz, a runner who had run in only one other race but came out of nowhere to win the Boston race. It was later proven that she had not run the entire course, actually running only about 400 yards to the finish line.

☐ c. After investigation that showed that she did not run the entire race, the 1980 Boston Marathon female winner, Rosie Ruiz, was stripped of her medal.

3. Choose the best one-sentence paraphrase for the following sentence from the article:

"She [the leading female runner] was often buried in a sea of male runners."

☐ a. The male runners often pushed aside the leading female runner.

☐ b. When the leading female runner died, she was often buried with male runners.

☐ c. The leading female runner was hard to see among the many male runners.

_____ Number of correct answers

Record your personal assessment of your work on the Critical Thinking Chart on page 136.

Critical Thinking

Put an X in the box next to the correct answer for questions 1, 2, and 3. Follow the directions provided for the other question.

1. From the article, you can predict that if anyone else tries to claim victory in the Boston Marathon without running the whole race,

☐ a. people will be more forgiving than they were to Ruiz.

☐ b. race officials will be ready with evidence to disprove the claim.

☐ c. he or she will probably get away with it because it has been several years since Rosie Ruiz pulled that trick.

2. What was the cause of the leading women runners' surprise at seeing Ruiz on the winner's stand?

☐ a. They hadn't seen Ruiz pass them in the race.

☐ b. They had never raced with Ruiz before.

☐ c. They hadn't thought that Ruiz was fast enough to win.

3. Of the following theme categories, which would this story fit into?

☐ a. A friend in need is a friend indeed.

☐ b. Blood is thicker than water.

☐ c. Cheaters never really win.

4. In which paragraphs did you find your information or details to answer question 2?

_____

_____ Number of correct answers

Record your personal assessment of your work on the Critical Thinking Chart on page 136.

Personal Response

How do you think you would feel if you had been the real winner of the Boston Marathon and saw Rosie Ruiz on the winner's stand?

_____

_____

_____

Self-Assessment

I'm proud of how I answered question # _____ in section _____

_____ because _____

_____

_____

_____

THE HITLER DIARIES HOAX

Adolph Hitler, founder of the German Nazi Party and Chancellor of the Third Reich, speaks at a party meeting in Munich in 1934.

The news stunned the world. On April 22, 1983, the German magazine *Stern* ran a huge headline. It read: HITLER'S DIARIES DISCOVERED. *Stern* claimed it had found 62 secret Hitler volumes. These covered the whole span of the German dictator's rule, from 1932 to 1945. *Stern* editors boasted that this was "the journalistic scoop of the post-World War II period."

2   Everyone wanted to know how *Stern* got the diaries. In response, reporter Gerd Heidemann told this story. Just before Hitler shot himself in 1945, he had ordered his personal papers flown out of Berlin. They were to be taken to his mountain retreat, but the plane crashed en route. A farmer found the diaries in the wrecked plane and hid them in a haystack for 38 years.

3   As *Stern's* top reporter on Hitler, Heidemann investigated the crash. It took him years of hard work, he claimed, but in the end, his efforts paid off. Heidemann found proof that some of the cargo from the doomed plane had survived. Next, he had tracked down the farmer who had the hidden diaries.

Beyond that, Hiedemann's story was a bit murky. He refused to say where he found the farmer, who the farmer was, or how Heidemann had convinced him to give up the diaries. Heidemann couldn't release this information, he said, because he had to protect his sources.

4   News of the diaries captured everyone's attention. As evil as Hitler had been, many people were fascinated by him. Since his death, he had been the subject of hundreds of books. He had also been a popular film subject. By 1980, there were 55 movies about him. So the diaries—if they were genuine—really would be a top story of the post-World War II period.

5   At first, many people believed the diaries were real. Certainly the editors at *Stern* thought they were. After all, Gerd Heidemann was one of their best reporters. "We have every reason to trust Heidemann thoroughly," said *Stern's* editor-in-chief Peter Koch.

6   Some historians were convinced, too. Hugh Trevor-Roper, a famous scholar, took a look at a few samples. "When I turned the pages of those volumes, my doubts gradually dissolved," he said. "I am now satisfied they are authentic."

7   Others came to the same conclusions. London's *Sunday Times* paid $400,000 for the right to print the diaries. In Italy, the magazine *Panorama* also paid a large sum for the diaries. In France, the weekly *Paris Match* did the same. And in the United States, *Newsweek* indicated interest. At the last minute, however, *Newsweek* editors had second thoughts and backed out.

8   That turned out to be a wise decision. Hitler's so-called diaries were a total hoax. Heidemann had gotten them from a man named Konrad Kujau. It is unclear whether Heidemann or Kujau masterminded the deception. Kujau was the one who actually wrote the diaries; Heidemann was the one who brought them to the public. In any case, both men were guilty of fraud.

9   At first, it appeared as though Heidemann and Kujau might get away with their crime. But soon doubts were raised. Skeptics quickly spotted errors in the diaries. Kujau had based the writings on a 1962 book by Max Domarus. So, of course, he repeated some of the same errors Domarus made. For instance, one entry has Hitler recalling a meeting with a top general. The general congratulated Hitler on his 50th year of military service. But Hitler was only 48 years old at the time. It was the general who had 50 years of service.

10   Kujau also repeated an error about the size of the crowd at one of Hitler's rallies. The real number was about 130,000 people. Both Domarus and Kujau pegged the number at half a million.

11   Even when confronted with these errors, the editors at *Stern* held their ground. They had too much invested in the story to give up without a fight. The magazine's reputation was on the line. Also, it had shelled out $4.1 million to buy the volumes. Editor-in-Chief Koch

Max Booms, president of the West German Federal Archives, holds a fake Hitler diary and the book from which the faked texts were copied.

flew to New York to defend the diaries. He spoke on national TV. "I expected the uproar," Koch said. "[I] expected that many incompetent people would denounce the diaries as fakes. This is because every other publishing house will envy our story."

12   But the evidence against the diaries kept mounting. Some people said they knew the diaries were phony even without reading them. First, they pointed out, there had never even been a rumor that Hitler had kept a diary. Rather, it was well known that Hitler hated to write. He almost always dictated his notes or letters to a secretary. Even his one book, *Mein Kampf*, had been dictated. So why would he have written so many entries over such a long time? And how could he have kept it a secret from everyone? James O'Donnell, an expert on Hitler, said, "It is beyond possibility that Hitler would have kept diaries without [anyone] knowing about it."

13   There were other problems. The handwriting in the diaries was all the same. But in 1944, Hitler barely survived a bombing attempt on his life. His writing arm was badly injured. The diaries had him penning an entry with no difficulty on the very day of his injury. Further, near the end of his life Hitler suffered from palsy, a nervous disease. Yet his handwriting showed no signs of a shaky hand.

14   The diaries themselves were the final giveaway. Kujau wrote the fake diaries in notebooks bound in imitation leather. Why would Hitler, who could afford the best, use such cheap notebooks? These books were supposedly kept over a 13-year span. Yet they did not differ from each other even a little bit. In addition, the pages were unstained, unworn. That was odd, since the early diaries had to be more than 50 years old. Finally, there came the chemical analysis. It removed all doubt. The paper and the binding had polyester fibers that did not come into use until after Hitler's death.

15   The fallout came fast and heavy. Heidemann was quickly fired. "We have kicked him out," announced Henri Nannen, the publisher of *Stern*. "I am now convinced he knew the diaries were forgeries." Peter Koch and three other *Stern* editors also were either fired or resigned. A red-faced Nannen confessed, "We have some reason to be ashamed." It took *Stern* several years to recover from the scandal and win back its readers.

16   In 1985, Gerd Heidemann and Konrad Kujau were tried for the swindle. They were both found guilty and sentenced to four years in prison. In his written confession, Kujau kept his sense of humor. At the end of his confession, in fine Hitler form, he added, "I admit having written the Hitler diaries. It took me two years to perfect my handwriting. [Signed] Adolf Hitler."

If you have been timed while reading this article, enter your reading time below. Then turn to the Words-per-Minute Table on page 133 and look up your reading speed (words per minute). Enter your reading speed on the graph on page 134.

Reading Time: Lesson 13

_____ : _____
Minutes   Seconds

A Finding the Main Idea

One statement below expresses the main idea of the article. One statement is too general, or too broad. The other statement explains only part of the article; it is too narrow. Label the statements using the following key:

M—Main Idea   **B—Too Broad**   **N—Too Narrow**

_____ 1. In 1983, publications all over the world were fooled by a reporter who falsely claimed that he had discovered diaries kept by Adolf Hitler.

_____ 2. Gerd Heidemann said the Hitler diaries had been hidden in a haystack in the German countryside for 38 years.

_____ 3. Even normally skeptical people believed in Gerd Heidemann's amazing 1983 discovery.

_____ Score 15 points for a correct M answer.

_____ Score 5 points for each correct B or N answer.

_____ **Total Score:** Finding the Main Idea

B Recalling Facts

How well do you remember the facts in the article? Put an X in the box next to the answer that correctly completes each statement about the article.

1. Gerd Hiedemann was a reporter for
   □ a. *Paris Match.*
   □ b. *Stern.*
   □ c. the *Sunday Times.*

2. According to Heidemann, a farmer found the diaries in
   □ a. a plane that had crashed.
   □ b. the knapsack of a courier who had been shot.
   □ c. the briefcase of general who stopped at the farm.

3. It turned out that Konrad Kujau based the diaries on a
   □ a. 1980 movie about Adolf Hitler.
   □ b. series of newspaper articles published from 1932 to 1945.
   □ c. 1962 book by Max Domarus.

4. The Hitler diaries were written in
   □ a. fancy leather-bound books.
   □ b. cheap notebooks bound in imitation leather.
   □ c. spiral-bound notebooks like students use.

5. The chemical analysis of the diaries found evidence of
   □ a. a glue that was not available during Hitler's life.
   □ b. an ink that was discovered after Hitler's death.
   □ c. polyester fibers that were used only after Hitler's death.

Score 5 points for each correct answer.

_____ **Total Score:** Recalling Facts

C Making Inferences

When you combine your own experience and information from a text to draw a conclusion that is not directly stated in that text, you are making an inference. Below are five statements that may or may not be inferences based on information in the article. Label the statements using the following key:

C—Correct Inference   F—Faulty Inference

_____ 1. Young, eager reporters, rather than experienced reporters, are usually assigned the most exciting news stories.

_____ 2. This article proves that readers should not trust the writings of any historians or reporters.

_____ 3. Before the diaries were exposed as frauds, Heidemann made a great deal of money.

_____ 4. What makes this deception illegal, not just immoral, is that the people who were fooled lost money on it.

_____ 5. Most people are interested in famous people's lives.

Score 5 points for each correct answer.

_____ **Total Score:** Making Inferences

D Using Words Precisely

Each numbered sentence below contains an underlined word or phrase from the article. Following the sentence are three definitions. One definition is closest to the meaning of the underlined word. One definition is opposite or nearly opposite. Label those two definitions using the following key. Do not label the remaining definition.

C—Closest   O—Opposite or Nearly Opposite

1. Beyond that, Hiedemann's story was a bit <u>murky</u>.

_____ a. comical

_____ b. crystal clear

_____ c. fuzzy

2. It is unclear whether Heidemann or Kujau <u>masterminded</u> the deception.

_____ a. were taken in by

_____ b. provided the idea for

_____ c. appreciated

3. "[I] expected that many <u>incompetent</u> people would denounce the diaries as fakes."

_____ a. skillful

_____ b. not interested

_____ c. not qualified

4. "[I] expected that many incompetent people would <u>denounce</u> the diaries as fakes."

_____ a. support

_____ b. attack

_____ c. enjoy

5. In 1985, Gerd Heidemann and Konrad Kujau were tried for the underlined(swindle).

_____ a. dishonest business transaction

_____ b. mistake

_____ c. honest activity

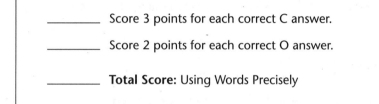

_____ Score 3 points for each correct C answer.

_____ Score 2 points for each correct O answer.

_____ **Total Score:** Using Words Precisely

Enter the four total scores in the spaces below, and add them together to find your Reading Comprehension Score. Then record your score on the graph on page 135.

Score	Question Type	Lesson 13
_____	Finding the Main Idea	
_____	Recalling Facts	
_____	Making Inferences	
_____	Using Words Precisely	
_____	**Reading Comprehension Score**	

Author's Approach

Put an X in the box next to the correct answer.

1. What does the author mean by the statement "*Stern* editors boasted that this was 'the journalistic scoop of the post-World War II period'"?

☐ a. The *Stern* editors felt that nothing of any importance had happened since World War II.

☐ b. The *Stern* editors were not at all concerned about the story's accuracy but cared only about reporting the story quickly.

☐ c. The editors of *Stern* were proud that their publication was the first one to report on this important story.

2. What is the author's purpose in writing "The Hitler Diaries Hoax"?

☐ a. To express an opinion about people who believe everything they read

☐ b. To inform the reader about a fascinating trick played on the public.

☐ c. To convey a mood of amusement and good humor

3. From the statements below, choose those that you believe the author would agree with.

☐ a. The Hitler diaries hoax was done so sloppily that it is no wonder it was eventually uncovered.

☐ b. The Hitler diaries hoax was planned and executed with the greatest possible attention to detail.

☐ c. The Hitler diaries hoax is one of the most significant events in modern history.

_____ Number of correct answers

Record your personal assessment of your work on the Critical Thinking Chart on page 136.

CRITICAL THINKING

Summarizing and Paraphrasing

Follow the directions provided for question 1. Put an X in the box next to the correct answer for questions 2 and 3.

1. Look for the important ideas and events in paragraphs 9 and 10. Summarize those paragraphs in one or two sentences.

_____

_____

_____

2. Read the statement about the article below. Then read the paraphrase of that statement. Choose the reason that best tells why the paraphrase does not say the same thing as the statement.

Statement: Heidemann said that he couldn't reveal certain information because he wanted to protect his sources.

Paraphrase: Heidemann said he couldn't answer questions such as where he found the farmer or who the farmer was because he was afraid that other people would steal his story.

☐ a. Paraphrase says too much.

☐ b. Paraphrase doesn't say enough.

☐ c. Paraphrase doesn't agree with the statement about the article.

3. Choose the best one-sentence paraphrase for the following sentence from the article:

"Heidemann found proof that some of the cargo from the doomed plane had survived."

☐ a. Heidemann was surprised that some of the plane's cargo had survived the crash.

☐ b. Heidemann found evidence that some things from the plane had survived the crash.

☐ c. Heidemann found some of the cargo that had survived the plane crash.

_____ Number of correct answers

Record your personal assessment of your work on the Critical Thinking Chart on page 136.

Critical Thinking

Put an X in the box next to the correct answer for questions 1 and 2. Follow the directions provided for the other questions.

1. Which of the following statements from the article is an opinion rather than a fact?

☐ a. "But in 1944, Hitler barely survived a bombing attempt on his life."

☐ b. "This is because every other publishing house will envy our story."

☐ c. "They were both found guilty and sentenced to four years in prison."

2. From the article, you can predict that if anyone else claims to have found diaries written by a famous person

☐ a. people will be less likely to believe him or her.

☐ b. people will accept the diaries as real, without questions.

☐ c. people will totally ignore the news.

3. Choose from the letters below to correctly complete the following statement. Write the letters on the lines.

In the article, _____ and _____ are alike because they both willingly took part in the deception.

a. Gerd Heidemann

b. Max Domarus

c. Konrad Kujau

4. Read paragraph 13. Then choose from the letters below to correctly complete the following statement Write the letters on the lines.

According to paragraph 13, _____ because _____.

a. Hitler had been hurt in a bombing attempt

b. Hitler had trouble with his handwriting

c. Hitler did not enjoy writing

5. What did you have to do to answer question 4?

☐ a. find a cause (why something happened)

☐ b. find a definition (what something means)

☐ c. find a summary (synthesized information)

_____ Number of correct answers

Record your personal assessment of your work on the Critical Thinking Chart on page 136.

Personal Response

What new question do you have about this topic?

_____

_____

_____

_____

Self-Assessment

From reading this article, I have learned

_____

_____

_____

_____

CRITICAL THINKING

CHARLES STUART

Charles Stuart and his wife Carol

Charles Stuart was bleeding heavily as he picked up his car phone and dialed the police.

2 "My wife's been shot," he cried into the phone. "I've been shot."

3 It was true. Both Charles "Chuck" Stuart and his wife Carol had been shot at close range as they sat in their car on the night of October 23, 1989. Stuart told the police dispatcher that he didn't know where he was. He and Carol, who was seven months pregnant, had just attended a birthing class at Boston's Brigham and Women's Hospital. Stuart said a man had climbed into their car as they stopped at an intersection. "He drove us, he made us go to an abandoned area," Stuart told dispatcher Gary McLaughlin.

4 "OK, sir," said McLaughlin, "can you see out the windows? Can you tell me where you are, please?"

5 "No," Stuart gasped, "I don't know. I don't see any signs. Oh, God."

6 McLaughlin kept Stuart on the line as Boston police frantically sped down the streets of the city in search of the injured couple. For 13 long minutes, McLaughlin comforted and encouraged Stuart, trying gently to coax information out of him. "Just calm down," he said to Stuart, "just

stay with me, I'm gonna get help to you, help is gonna be on the way."

7   After several minutes Stuart cried, "Oh, man, I'm gonna pass out…. It hurts, and my wife has stopped gurgling, she's stopped breathing."

8   "Chuck," said McLaughlin, "I'm gonna get assistance to you, buddy."

9   At last, the police did find Stuart's blue Toyota Cressida with Stuart slumped in the driver's seat and his wife unconscious in the blood-spattered seat beside him. Both were in bad shape. At the hospital, doctors delivered the baby—Christopher—with an emergency Caesarian section. A few hours after that, Carol Stuart died. Her husband and infant son remained in critical condition.

10   The people of Boston were appalled by the vicious and random nature of the crime. Charles and Carol Stuart had both grown up in the Boston area, children of working class families. They had worked hard at their professions, and they had succeeded. He had become office manager of a fashionable fur store and she was a tax lawyer. It was unimaginable that something like this would happen to such good people.

11   The details of the crime shocked everyone. According to Charles, a black man wielding a gun had jumped into their car when they stopped at an intersection not far from the hospital. Stuart described the man as having a "raspy, singsong" voice and "splotchy" facial hair. He wore a black baseball cap, black jogging jacket with red stripes, and black driving gloves with exposed knuckles.

12   The man ordered Charles to start driving, directing him through a confusing series of turns into a poor neighborhood called Mission Hill. He then demanded Carol give him all the jewelry she was wearing, including her wedding ring. At that point, said Charles, the gunman noticed the Stuarts' car phone and suddenly became nervous. He accused the couple of being undercover cops. In his anger and fear, he shot them.

A view of the Stuart grave covered with flowers

The first bullet hit Carol in the head. The second struck Charles in his abdomen. After that, the man jumped out of the car and disappeared into the night.

13 As the people of Boston reeled with horror and outrage over this story, arrangements were made for Carol's funeral. Charles had undergone extensive surgery and was far too weak to attend the service. Still, from his hospital bed, he managed to write a poignant letter for the occasion. "Good night, sweet wife, my love," he wrote. "Now you sleep away from me. I will never again know the feeling of your hand in mine, but I will always feel you...." The 800 mourners at the funeral sobbed openly as the letter was read aloud by the best man from Charles and Carol's wedding.

14 The pain was not over yet. Seventeen days after Christopher was born, the baby worsened and slipped toward death. Charles asked to be wheeled to his son's bedside to hold him once before he died. After Christopher's death, Charles spent four more weeks in the hospital recovering from his wounds.

15 Meanwhile, the Boston police launched an all-out search for the gunman. The mayor put all available police officers on the case. In Mission Hill, virtually every African-American man came under suspicion. Police stopped up to 150 such men each day, asking them questions and searching them for weapons.

16 At last, police settled on William Bennett, a young man with a long criminal record. Reports had come in that he was boasting to friends about killing Carol Stuart. When shown Bennett's picture, Charles Stuart had a "strong physical reaction." And on December 28, Charles picked Bennett out of a police lineup.

17 It looked as though the police had found their man. But on January 3, 1990—less than a week after the lineup—Charles's brother Matthew went to the police with a stunning story. William Bennett was not the killer, said Matthew. Rather, it was Charles Stuart who was guilty of murder.

18 Matthew explained that Charles had asked to meet him in Mission Hill on the night of the murder. Matthew had agreed, parking on the street with his car window open as Charles had requested. At the appointed time, Charles had driven up, thrown Carol's purse into Matthew's car, and said, "Take this to Revere [where Matthew lived]." It was dark; Matthew saw "something" on the seat next to Charles, but he didn't know it was Carol and he certainly didn't know she had been shot. Matthew claimed that he simply thought Charles was setting up some kind of robbery scheme.

19 Back home in Revere, Matthew opened Carol's purse and found the gun and the jewelry. Later, when he heard about the shootings, he threw both the purse and its contents in the river. But, he explained to police, he kept Carol's wedding ring to prove his story. And indeed, Matthew then produced the ring.

20 Suddenly, a whole new scenario of the crime emerged. It was discovered that Charles Stuart had not been happy about his wife's pregnancy. Furthermore, he had hoped to open a restaurant soon and could have used the insurance money from his wife's death to finance the business. He had therefore concocted an elaborate plan, making up a black gunman and giving himself a life-threatening wound to throw police off the track.

21 The day after Matthew Stuart came forward, police went to question Charles. But he was still one step ahead of them. Early that morning, he drove to the Tobin Bridge, a huge bridge that spans Boston's Mystic River. There the man who had killed his wife and child, traumatized a city, and carved racial wounds throughout the community, ended the story by jumping to his own death.

If you have been timed while reading this article, enter your reading time below. Then turn to the Words-per-Minute Table on page 133 and look up your reading speed (words per minute). Enter your reading speed on the graph on page 134.

Reading Time: Lesson 14

_____ : _____
Minutes   *Seconds*

A | Finding the Main Idea

One statement below expresses the main idea of the article. One statement is too general, or too broad. The other statement explains only part of the article; it is too narrow. Label the statements using the following key:

M—Main Idea   **B—Too Broad**   **N—Too Narrow**

_____ 1. The sad case of Charles and Carol Stuart proves that human beings are capable of hideous crimes.

_____ 2. Charles Stuart killed his wife and wounded himself in a deception that finally unraveled and ended in his own suicide.

_____ 3. On October 23, 1989, Charles Stuart frantically called the police dispatcher to report that he and his pregnant wife had both been shot by an unknown assailant.

_____ Score 15 points for a correct M answer.

_____ Score 5 points for each correct B or N answer.

_____ **Total Score:** Finding the Main Idea

B | Recalling Facts

How well do you remember the facts in the article? Put an X in the box next to the answer that correctly completes each statement about the article.

1. While the police dispatcher comforted Charles Stuart on the phone, other police
   - ☐ a. tried to save the Stuarts' unborn baby.
   - ☐ b. flew helicopters looking for the Stuarts.
   - ☐ c. drove through Boston streets looking for the Stuarts.

2. Carol Stuart was
   - ☐ a. a buyer for a clothing store.
   - ☐ b. a tax lawyer.
   - ☐ c. the office manager of a fur store.

3. According to Charles, the gunman became nervous when he saw
   - ☐ a. the Stuarts' car phone.
   - ☐ b. the gun that Charles Stuart always carried.
   - ☐ c. that Carol was pregnant.

4. All of the men the police stopped and searched were
   - ☐ a. tall and thin.
   - ☐ b. African Americans.
   - ☐ c. ex-convicts.

5. Charles Stuart killed his wife because
   - ☐ a. he wanted to marry someone else.
   - ☐ b. she had asked him to kill her because she was so ill.
   - ☐ c. he wanted the insurance money from his wife's death.

Score 5 points for each correct answer.

_____ **Total Score:** Recalling Facts

Making Inferences

When you combine your own experience and information from a text to draw a conclusion that is not directly stated in that text, you are making an inference. Below are five statements that may or may not be inferences based on information in the article. Label the statements using the following key:

C—Correct Inference   **F—Faulty Inference**

_____ 1. People resent being stopped and searched just because of their race and gender.

_____ 2. In 1989, car phones were less common than they are today.

_____ 3. Matthew Stuart was totally unwilling to become part of any illegal scheme.

_____ 4. After Matthew learned about the shootings, he decided that it was dangerous for him to keep Carol's purse.

_____ 5. When victims identify a suspect in a lineup, police know for sure that the suspect is the criminal they were seeking.

Score 5 points for each correct answer.

_____ **Total Score:** Making Inferences

D **Using Words Precisely**

Each numbered sentence below contains an underlined word or phrase from the article. Following the sentence are three definitions. One definition is closest to the meaning of the underlined word. One definition is opposite or nearly opposite. Label those two definitions using the following key. Do not label the remaining definition.

C—Closest   **O—Opposite or Nearly Opposite**

1. The people of Boston were <u>appalled</u> by the vicious and random nature of the crime.

_____ a. pleased

_____ b. fascinated

_____ c. horrified

2. Still, from his hospital bed, he managed to write a <u>poignant</u> letter for the occasion.

_____ a. touching and sad

_____ b. happy-go-lucky

_____ c. long

3. He had therefore <u>concocted</u> an elaborate plan.

_____ a. read about

_____ b. destroyed

_____ c. invented

4. He had therefore concocted an <u>elaborate</u> plan.

_____ a. simple

_____ b. complicated

_____ c. cruel

5. There the man who had...<u>traumatized</u> a city...ended the story by jumping to his own death.

_____ a. praised

_____ b. soothed

_____ c. deeply shocked

_____ Score 3 points for each correct C answer.

_____ Score 2 points for each correct O answer.

_____ **Total Score:** Using Words Precisely

Enter the four total scores in the spaces below, and add them together to find your Reading Comprehension Score. Then record your score on the graph on page 135.

Score	Question Type	Lesson 14
_____	Finding the Main Idea	
_____	Recalling Facts	
_____	Making Inferences	
_____	Using Words Precisely	
_____	**Reading Comprehension Score**	

Author's Approach

Put an X in the box next to the correct answer.

1. The author uses the first sentence of the article to
   - ☐ a. persuade the reader to buy a car phone.
   - ☐ b. describe the qualities of Charles Stuart that made him a good husband.
   - ☐ c. arouse the reader's curiosity about Charles Stuart's situation.

2. Judging by statements from the article "Charles Stuart," you can conclude that the author wants the reader to think that Charles Stuart
   - ☐ a. committed this crime at the spur of the moment, without planning it.
   - ☐ b. was terribly upset at the death of his son.
   - ☐ c. would stop at nothing to collect his wife's insurance.

3. This statement, "Charles and Carol Stuart had both grown up in the Boston area, children of working class families," means that Charles and Carol grew up among people who
   - ☐ a. worked hard for a living and were neither rich nor poor.
   - ☐ b. were wealthy and had a lot of class.
   - ☐ c. were unbelievably poor.

4. What does the author imply by saying "Matthew claimed that he simply thought Charles was setting up some kind of robbery scheme"?
   - ☐ a. Matthew had no real objection to helping with a robbery.
   - ☐ b. Matthew was glad that Charles only wanted to rob, not kill.
   - ☐ c. Matthew was an experienced robber.

_____ Number of correct answers

Record your personal assessment of your work on the Critical Thinking Chart on page 136.

CRITICAL THINKING

Summarizing and Paraphrasing

Follow the directions provided for questions 1 and 2. Put an X in the box next to the correct answer for question 3.

1. Complete the following one-sentence summary of the article using the lettered phrases from the phrase bank below. Write the letters on the lines.

> **Phrase Bank:**
> a. a description of the night of the murder of Carol Stuart
> b. the death of Charles Stuart
> c. what happened after the Stuarts were found by police

The article about Charles Stuart begins with _____, goes on to explain _____, and ends with _____.

2. Reread paragraph 15 in the article. Below, write a summary of the paragraph in no more than 25 words.

_____

_____

_____

_____

Reread your summary and decide whether it covers the important ideas in the paragraph. Next, try to shorten the summary to 15 words or less without leaving out any essential information. Write this summary below.

_____

_____

3. Choose the sentence that correctly restates the following sentence from the article:

"Suddenly, a whole new scenario of the crime emerged."

☐ a. All at once, the criminals came forward into the scene.

☐ b. Suddenly, the scene of the crime looked different.

☐ c. All at once, a new way of looking at the crime became clear.

> _____ Number of correct answers
>
> Record your personal assessment of your work on the Critical Thinking Chart on page 136.

Critical Thinking

Put an X in the box next to the correct answer for questions 1, 3, and 4. Follow the directions provided for the other questions.

1. Which of the following statements from the article is an opinion rather than a fact?

☐ a. "It was unimaginable that something like this would happen to such good people."

☐ b. "And on December 28, Charles picked Bennett out of a police lineup."

☐ c. "Later, when he heard about the shootings, he threw both the purse and its contents in the river."

CRITICAL THINKING

2. Choose from the letters below to correctly complete the following statement. Write the letters on the lines.

In the article, _____ and _____ are alike because they both believed Charles Stuart's story.

a. all the members of the Stuart family

b. the people of Boston

c. the Boston police

3. What was the effect of Charles's story that a black man had attacked him and his wife in the Mission Hill district?

☐ a. Police stopped people from entering or leaving the Mission Hill district.

☐ b. Police arrested many African-American men for the crime.

☐ c. Police stopped and searched hundreds of African-American men in the Mission Hill district.

4. What did you have to do to answer question 2?

☐ a. find an opinion (what someone thinks about something)

☐ b. find a purpose (why something is done)

☐ c. find a comparison (how things are the same)

_____ Number of correct answers

Record your personal assessment of your work on the Critical Thinking Chart on page 136.

Personal Response

1. Why do you think Matthew Stuart went to the police with his information about his brother's crime?

_____

_____

_____

_____

2. How do you think Matthew Stuart felt when he realized that his brother was really a killer and not a victim?

_____

_____

_____

Self-Assessment

I'm proud of how I answered question # _____ in section _____

_____ because _____

_____

_____

_____

CRITICAL THINKING

Compare and Contrast

Think about the articles you have read in Unit Two. Pick four articles that describe especially unusual deceptions. Write the titles in the first column of the chart below. Use information you learned from the articles to fill in the empty boxes in the chart.

Title	Which part of the deception did you find most surprising?	Why do you think each deceiver decided to fool his or her victims?	How did each deception affect the lives of its victims?

Which of these deceivers would you most like to meet? If you could meet him or her, what questions would you ask? _____

_____

_____

Words-per-Minute Table

Unit Two

Directions: If you were timed while reading an article, refer to the Reading Time you recorded in the box at the end of the article. Use this words-per-minute table to determine your reading speed for that article. Then plot your reading speed on the graph on page 134.

Lesson No. of Words	8 1117	9 1157	10 1055	11 1301	12 1106	13 1136	14 1148	Seconds
1:30	745	771	703	867	737	757	765	90
1:40	670	694	633	781	664	682	689	100
1:50	609	631	575	710	603	620	626	110
2:00	559	579	528	651	553	568	574	120
2:10	516	534	487	600	510	524	530	130
2:20	479	496	452	558	474	487	492	140
2:30	447	463	422	520	442	454	459	150
2:40	419	434	396	488	415	426	431	160
2:50	394	408	372	459	390	401	405	170
3:00	372	386	352	434	369	379	383	180
3:10	353	365	333	411	349	359	363	190
3:20	335	347	317	390	332	341	344	200
3:30	319	331	301	372	316	325	328	210
3:40	305	316	288	355	302	310	313	220
3:50	291	302	275	339	289	296	299	230
4:00	279	289	264	325	277	284	287	240
4:10	268	278	253	312	265	273	276	250
4:20	258	267	243	300	255	262	265	260
4:30	248	257	234	289	246	252	255	270
4:40	239	248	226	279	237	243	246	280
4:50	231	239	218	269	229	235	238	290
5:00	223	231	211	260	221	227	230	300
5:10	216	224	204	252	214	220	222	310
5:20	209	217	198	244	207	213	215	320
5:30	203	210	192	237	201	207	209	330
5:40	197	204	186	230	195	200	203	340
5:50	191	198	181	223	190	195	197	350
6:00	186	193	176	217	184	189	191	360
6:10	181	188	171	211	179	184	186	370
6:20	176	183	167	205	175	179	181	380
6:30	172	178	162	200	170	175	177	390
6:40	168	174	158	195	166	170	172	400
6:50	163	169	154	190	162	166	168	410
7:00	160	165	151	186	158	162	164	420
7:10	156	161	147	182	154	159	160	430
7:20	152	158	144	177	151	155	157	440
7:30	149	154	141	173	147	151	153	450
7:40	146	151	138	170	144	148	150	460
7:50	143	148	135	166	141	145	147	470
8:00	140	145	132	163	138	142	144	480

Minutes and Seconds

Plotting Your Progress: Reading Speed

Unit Two

Directions: If you were timed while reading an article, write your words-per-minute rate for that article in the box under the number of the lesson. Then plot your reading speed on the graph by putting a small X on the line directly above the number of the lesson, across from the number of words per minute you read. As you mark your speed for each lesson, graph your progress by drawing a line to connect the X's.

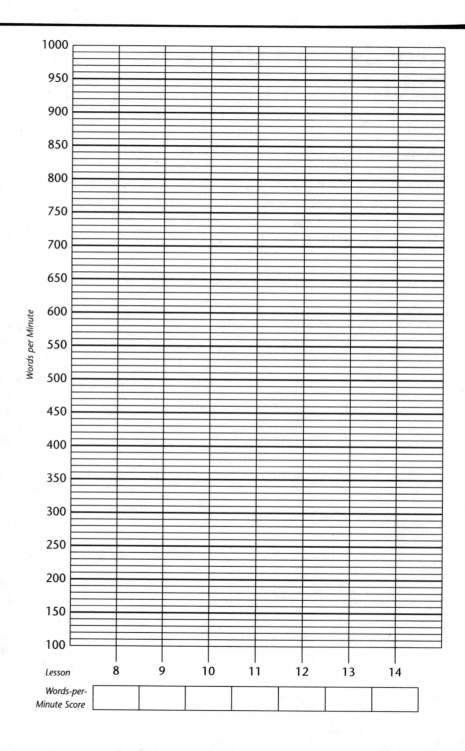

Plotting Your Progress: Reading Comprehension

Unit Two

Directions: Write your Reading Comprehension score for each lesson in the box under the number of the lesson. Then plot your score on the graph by putting a small X on the line directly above the number of the lesson and across from the score you earned. As you mark your score for each lesson, graph your progress by drawing a line to connect the X's.

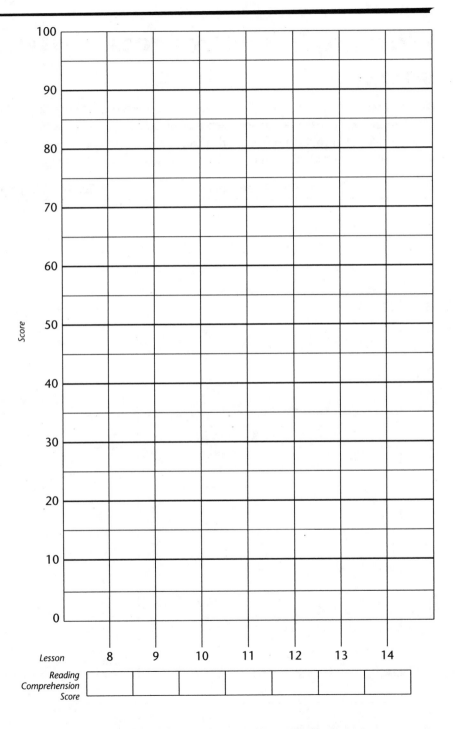

Score

Lesson | 8 | 9 | 10 | 11 | 12 | 13 | 14

Reading Comprehension Score

Plotting Your Progress: Critical Thinking

Unit Two

Directions: Work with your teacher to evaluate your responses to the Critical Thinking questions for each lesson. Then fill in the appropriate spaces in the chart below. For each lesson and each type of Critical Thinking question, do the following: Mark a minus sign (–) in the box to indicate areas in which you feel you could improve. Mark a plus sign (+) to indicate areas in which you feel you did well. Mark a minus-slash-plus sign (–/+) to indicate areas in which you had mixed success. Then write any comments you have about your performance, including ideas for improvement.

Lesson	Author's Approach	Summarizing and Paraphrasing	Critical Thinking
8			
9			
10			
11			
12			
13			
14			

UNIT THREE

PRICELESS FAKES

Young Woman with a Jug, *an original work painted by Jan Vermeer about 1662*

"**P**riceless" works of art are not really priceless. They all have real dollar prices attached to them—and what prices! In 1987, a Japanese buyer spent a staggering $40 million for Vincent van Gogh's *Sunflowers*. In 1990, van Gogh's *Portrait of Dr. Gachet* sold for an even more incredible $82.5 million. These days, great works of art routinely sell for very high prices.

2   In another sense, of course, such pieces *are* priceless. That is, their value is beyond price. After all, van Gogh produced only a limited number of masterpieces. Or did he produce what is credited to him? Annet Tellegen, a leading van Gogh expert, believes that about one out of 15 "authentic" van Goghs is a forgery. That is, it is a work done in van Gogh's style and with van Gogh's technique. But these paintings were *not* painted by the master himself. Rather, they were created by professional forgers.

3   Thomas Hoving makes an even bolder claim. From 1967 to 1978, Hoving served as director of the Metropolitan Museum in New York City. Hoving says that thousands of works in the museum's collection are "phonies."

4   Clearly, then, art forgery is big business. But who are the forgers? It is not a crime just anyone can commit. It takes the enormous daring of a daylight bank robber. It also takes tremendous talent and knowledge. A forger must be a decent artist himself and must know every brush or chisel stroke of the real artist. The forger has to be a pretty good chemist, as well. He or she must mix exactly the right pigments to get the precise colors of the original. Further, he must use exactly the right chemicals to "age" the work convincingly.

5   Tom Keating was one such forger. He studied art in London but failed to earn his diploma. He found work restoring old paintings. The work gave him insight into the styles and sensibilities of the masters. Keating soon turned to forgery, and he eventually forged the work of more than 100 artists.

6   Keating was good enough to get away with his trickery for a long time. He worked hard to produce works of art that mirrored exactly the true artist's style. To make the ink he needed for a Rembrandt drawing, for example, he painstakingly mixed the brown juice of simmered apples with a touch of instant coffee. Keating could also be playful. He often wrote the word *fake* in his forgeries, then covered over the word with a layer of paint.

7   Although Keating was poor, he insisted his motivation was not money. He just hated to see art dealers making so much money off the talents of others. "It was not for gain," said Keating when he finally confessed his fraud. "[I produced the frauds] simply as a protest against merchants who make capital out of those I am proud to call my brother artists, both living and dead." Keating was eventually arrested, but all charges were dropped because of his poor health. Tom Keating died on February 12, 1984.

8   Hans van Meegeren was a slightly different kind of forger: he was a specialist. His notoriety came from forging works of one artist, the 17th century Dutch master Johannes Vermeer. Van Meegeren, like Keating, studied art and worked as an art restorer. His own creations sold fairly well. But the art critics declared his work mediocre and lacked originality. This greatly angered van Meegeren. Forging Vermeer was his way of getting even.

9   Van Meegeren took great care producing his fake art. He used just the right canvas. He mixed his paint colors just as Vermeer had done. For example, he used crushed insect shells for crimson. He also discovered the exact formula for properly aging his fakes. Part of his secret was baking the painting at 220 degrees for two hours.

Alceo Dossena, an Italian artist whose imitations of master sculptures have fooled the experts, works on a piece of sculpture in his studio.

10   In 1937, van Meegeren brought forward one of his paintings, claiming it was a lost Vermeer that had just been discovered in a Paris apartment. Called *Christ at Emmaus*, it was a sensational piece of art. It fooled everyone, even the top critics. One expert said the work was "of the highest art, the highest beauty." Another declared that it was "*the masterpiece of Johannes Vermeer.*" Better yet, a Dutch museum bought the fake for $270,000.

11   Over the next few years, van Meegeren arranged to have more Vermeers "found." They were all scooped up by private buyers or museums. During World War II, one fake found its way into the hands of the German Nazis. After the war, the Dutch police traced the painting back to van Meegeren. Still believing the painting was the work of Vermeer, Dutch police arrested van Meegeren and charged him with selling a national treasure to the enemy.

12   At that point, van Meegeren saw only one way to save himself. He confessed that the painting wasn't a national treasure—it was a forgery! No one believed him. To prove it, van Meegeren painted another fake while the police watched. At last, the police were convinced. They dropped the charge of selling a national treasure and instead charged Van Meegeren with forgery. He was found guilty and sentenced to a year in jail.

13   Although he ended up in prison, van Meegeren had gotten his revenge. He had embarrassed all the art critics. He became a folk hero to the Dutch people, but he didn't live to enjoy his fame. Hans van Meegeren died less than two months after being sent to prison.

14   Alceo Dossena didn't forge paintings; he forged sculpture. And he was exceedingly good at it. His works appeared in most of the world's major museums. Dossena produced beautiful sculpture from all periods of the ancient world. He created flawless fakes from the period known as the Renaissance. In today's money, the value of his works sold to Americans was estimated to be between $20 million and $60 million.

15   Dossena, who died in 1937, maintained that he wasn't a crook. He himself never claimed that his works were genuine. He said he'd simply made them as pieces for decoration. "I am not a forger," he once said. "I never copied works. I simply reconstructed them." Still, he was so good that art dealers had no trouble selling them as the real thing.

16   Museums that were duped by Dossena were often reluctant to admit it. They didn't want to look foolish. Also, they didn't want the value of their "masterpieces" destroyed. In 1924, for example, the Museum of Fine Arts in Boston bought a marble coffin for $100,000. The museum thought it was a rare 15th century work by Mino da Fiesole. Actually, it was a 20th century work by Alceo Dossena. Despite the fact that it was soon revealed as a fake, the museum kept it. Rather sheepishly, a spokesman said that whatever its origin, "it is a beautiful object."

17   Dossena produced hundreds of fakes. But he never made much money. Art dealers were the ones who got rich off his talent. One dealer sold a fake sculpture for $150,000 but gave Dossena just $7,500. Another dealer sold a work for more than $360,000 but passed only $1,500 on to Dossena.

18   The forgeries of Keating, van Meegeren, and Dossena are still around. There may even be one in a museum near you. It seems that such fakes have a fascination all their own. In 1990, the British Museum mounted a show entitled "Fake!" The museum collected all sorts of fakes and forgeries and put them on display. The public lapped it up. "Fake!" broke all the museum's attendance records.

If you have been timed while reading this article, enter your reading time below. Then turn to the Words-per-Minute Table on page 195 and look up your reading speed (words per minute). Enter your reading speed on the graph on page 196.

Reading Time: Lesson 15

_____ : _____
Minutes   Seconds

A   Finding the Main Idea

One statement below expresses the main idea of the article. One statement is too general, or too broad. The other statement explains only part of the article; it is too narrow. Label the statements using the following key:

M—Main Idea   **B—Too Broad**   **N—Too Narrow**

_____ 1. Alceo Dossena was a gifted sculptor who made much less money than the dealers who sold his work.

_____ 2. Artists who produce works that are credited to more famous artists do so for various reasons and with varying levels of success.

_____ 3. There are many works of art whose creators are difficult, if not impossible, to identify accurately.

_____ Score 15 points for a correct M answer.

_____ Score 5 points for each correct B or N answer.

_____ **Total Score:** Finding the Main Idea

B   Recalling Facts

How well do you remember the facts in the article? Put an X in the box next to the answer that correctly completes each statement about the article.

1. One leading van Gogh expert estimated that one in 15 van Gogh paintings
   - ☐ a. will be sold for a very high price.
   - ☐ b. is a forgery.
   - ☐ c. is in the Metropolitan Museum in New York City.

2. To be a good forger of paintings, a man or woman must
   - ☐ a. be good at both art and chemistry.
   - ☐ b. get the cooperation of dishonest art dealers.
   - ☐ c. be motivated by anger at art critics.

3. All three forgers discussed in this article
   - ☐ a. got into trouble with the authorities because of their forgeries.
   - ☐ b. created fake van Gogh paintings.
   - ☐ c. died in prison.

4. Hans van Meegeren admitted he was a forger when
   - ☐ a. someone else took credit for his work.
   - ☐ b. he was charged with selling a national treasure to his country's enemy.
   - ☐ c. an art critic wrote that his work looked suspicious.

5. It's safe to say that
   - ☐ a. very few forgeries are still in art museums.
   - ☐ b. forgeries can be found in a large number of museums.
   - ☐ c. when museums discover forgeries in their collections, they get rid of them instantly and with public explanations.

Score 5 points for each correct answer.

_____ **Total Score:** Recalling Facts

C | Making Inferences

When you combine your own experience and information from a text to draw a conclusion that is not directly stated in that text, you are making an inference. Below are five statements that may or may not be inferences based on information in the article. Label the statements using the following key:

C—Correct Inference   F—Faulty Inference

_____ 1. Many people who become forgers learn the tricks of the forgery trade while working as art restorers.

_____ 2. The typical art forger, like the three described in this article, is found out during his or her lifetime.

_____ 3. You are likely to make more money as an art dealer than as an artist.

_____ 4. The British Museum has more fakes in its collection than does any other museum.

_____ 5. Holland has laws governing the buying and selling of national treasures.

Score 5 points for each correct answer.

_____ **Total Score:** Making Inferences

D | Using Words Precisely

Each numbered sentence below contains an underlined word or phrase from the article. Following the sentence are three definitions. One definition is closest to the meaning of the underlined word. One definition is opposite or nearly opposite. Label those two definitions using the following key. Do not label the remaining definition.

C—Closest   O—Opposite or Nearly Opposite

1. That is, it is a work done in van Gogh's style and with van Gogh's technique.

_____ a. method

_____ b. disorderliness

_____ c. reliability

2. Further, he must use exactly the right chemicals to "age" the work convincingly.

_____ a. in a way that makes a thing seem old

_____ b. in a way that creates doubt

_____ c. in such a way as to persuade others

3. His notoriety came from forging works of one artist, the 17th century Dutch master Johannes Vermeer.

_____ a. good reputation

_____ b. ill fame

_____ c. income

4. He <u>confessed</u> that the painting wasn't a national treasure—it was a forgery!

_____ a. admitted

_____ b. repeated

_____ c. denied

5. It seems that such fakes have a <u>fascination</u> all their own.

_____ a. fame

_____ b. drabness

_____ c. attraction

_____ Score 3 points for each correct C answer.

_____ Score 2 points for each correct O answer.

_____ **Total Score:** Using Words Precisely

Enter the four total scores in the spaces below, and add them together to find your Reading Comprehension Score. Then record your score on the graph on page 197.

Score	Question Type	Lesson 15
_____	Finding the Main Idea	
_____	Recalling Facts	
_____	Making Inferences	
_____	Using Words Precisely	
_____	**Reading Comprehension Score**	

Author's Approach

Put an X in the box next to the correct answer.

1. The main purpose of the first paragraph is to

☐ a. explain who Vincent van Gogh was.

☐ b. establish the fact that art is worth a great deal of money.

☐ c. identify the highest price ever paid for a work of art.

2. What is the author's purpose in writing "Priceless Fakes"?

☐ a. To encourage the reader to have his or her art collection examined by experts to identify any possible forgeries

☐ b. To inform the reader about an interesting aspect of the art scene

☐ c. To persuade art forgers to give up an activity that causes disappointment, embarrassment, and financial pain for others

3. From statements in the article "Priceless Fakes," you can conclude that the author wants the reader to think that

☐ a. people who work for museums are easily fooled.

☐ b. even experts can be fooled by gifted forgers.

☐ c. almost anyone can forge "classic" works of art.

4. The author develops this topic mainly by

☐ a. retelling personal experiences.

☐ b. using his or her imagination and creativity.

☐ c. reporting different aspects of the same problem.

_____ Number of correct answers

Record your personal assessment of your work on the Critical Thinking Chart on page 198.

CRITICAL THINKING

Summarizing and Paraphrasing

Put an X in the box next to the correct answer.

1. Below are summaries of the article. Choose the summary that says all the most important things about the article but in the fewest words.

☐ a. Tom Keating forged paintings by over 100 artists to protest how much money the dealers made off artists. Another painter, Hans van Meegeren, forged many works in the style of Johannes Vermeer to get even with critics who disliked his own style. Alceo Dossena created fake Renaissance sculpture simply because he was good at it.

☐ b. The stories of three art forgers—Tom Keating, Hans van Meegeren, and Alceo Dossena—illustrate how much effort the forgers put into their creations and how many other motives besides money drove them.

☐ c. Tom Keating, Hans van Meegeren, and Alceo Dossena are three typical art forgers who were caught.

2. Read the statement about the article below. Then read the paraphrase of that statement. Choose the reason that best tells why the paraphrase does not say the same thing as the statement.

Statement: Although he ended up in prison, van Meegeren had gotten his revenge.

Paraphrase: Van Meegeren got his revenge when he went to prison.

☐ a. Paraphrase says too much.

☐ b. Paraphrase doesn't say enough.

☐ c. Paraphrase doesn't agree with the statement about the article.

3. Choose the best one-sentence paraphrase for the following sentence from the article:

"[I did it] simply as a protest against merchants who make capital out of those I am proud to call my brother artists, both living and dead."

☐ a. I did it because I think it is unfair for salespeople to make money off the work of my fellow artists.

☐ b. I did it to point out that it is wrong for salespeople to capitalize the names of artists of today and the past.

☐ c. I did it to protest against salespeople who make works of art into things the artists, alive or dead, never intended.

_____ Number of correct answers

Record your personal assessment of your work on the Critical Thinking Chart on page 198.

Critical Thinking

Put an X in the box next to the correct answer for questions 1 and 2. Follow the directions provided for the other questions.

1. From what the article told about the profits some art dealers made on Dossena's works, you can predict that

☐ a. no other art dealers can make profits without bending the truth about the works they sell.

☐ b. all other art dealers will drive these dishonest dealers out of the business.

☐ c. some other art dealers will misrepresent the work of unknown artists simply to make money.

2. Using the information in paragraph 2, you can predict that

☐ a. art forgers will not imitate any great artists except Vincent van Gogh.

☐ b. van Gogh experts will find it easy to spot van Gogh forgeries.

☐ c. some works now believed to be by van Gogh will be identified as fakes.

3. Choose from the letters below to correctly complete the following statement Write the letters on the lines.

In the article, _____ and _____ are alike because they both forged paintings.

a. Tom Keating

b. Hans van Meegeren

c. Alceo Dossena

4. Which paragraphs from the article provide evidence that supports your answer to question 3?

_____

_____ Number of correct answers

Record your personal assessment of your work on the Critical Thinking Chart on page 198.

Personal Response

1. How do you think you would feel if you discovered you had spent a great deal of money on art that was a forgery?

_____

_____

_____

2. What new question do you have about this topic?

_____

_____

_____

Self-Assessment

1. Before reading this article, I already knew

_____

_____

_____

2. From reading this article, I learned

_____

_____

_____

KATHERINE ANN POWER
Life on the Run

American college students were politically active in the 1960s and early 1970s. Here, students from Kent State University in Ohio protest on the Ellipse in Washington, D.C.

As a teenager, Katherine Ann Power was her family's "pride and joy." She was a star student at Marycrest, a private girl's school in Denver. She wrote a youth column for the *Denver Post* and spent her spare time reading, sewing, and cooking. She even won the Betty Crocker Homemaker Award. Yet somehow, at age 21, Power ended up on the FBI's Most Wanted List. In 1970, she became a fugitive who survived only by cutting all contact with her family and going deep into hiding.

2   The transformation in Power's life began when she entered Brandeis University just west of Boston. The year was 1967. The Vietnam War was escalating and college campuses across the country were becoming hotbeds of anti-war sentiment. Power soon joined the movement. At first, she was no more radical than other college students. She went to rallies, speeches, and protest marches. But in the spring of 1970, Power's notions of love and peace became tangled up with thoughts of violence and crime. She decided she should take bold—

even criminal—action to protest the war. She built up a store of weapons in her apartment and looked for a chance to use them.

3   Her chance came in the fall of 1970. By then, she had joined forces with two equally radical students: her roommate Susan Saxe and an ex-convict named Stanley Bond. Bond was attending Brandeis as part of a program to give ex-convicts a good education. He and two of his prison contacts set up a bank robbery in Brighton, Massachusetts. Saxe and Power agreed to take part in the heist. Their ill-conceived plan was to steal enough money to buy more weapons for fellow radicals.

4   Power's role in the robbery was to drive the getaway car. She was sitting in that car when a Boston police officer named William Schroeder interrupted the robbery. One of the ex-convicts shot Schroeder, who died of his wounds a few days later. In the eyes of the law, all participants in the robbery were guilty of murder. The three men involved were caught, but Saxe and Power got away.

5   And so began Katherine Ann Power's life on the run. She and Saxe went first to Philadelphia, then south to Atlanta. After that, they crisscrossed the country, taking care to keep low profiles and to avoid any contact with the law. For a while they lived in a Connecticut commune. Later they moved to Kentucky. Somewhere along the line, Power took on a new identity, calling herself Sheila Mae Kelly.

6   In 1974, Power and Saxe went their separate ways. Soon after, Saxe was arrested. Her capture frightened Power, who became even more determined to elude police. She drifted from city to city, taking menial jobs that required no references. She made up new names for herself as she went along.

7   In 1977, Power got hold of the birth certificate of a baby named Alice Metzinger who had died long before. Had the child lived, she would have been about Power's age. Power took on Metzinger's identity. Using the birth certificate as identification, she obtained a driver's license and social security number. For the next 16 years, Power masqueraded as Metzinger. In 1979 she had a son, whom she named Jaime. The following year, she fell in love with a man named Ron Duncan. He joined her as she moved from town to town.

8   Eventually Power and Duncan bought a house together, settling in Lebanon, Oregon. Power got a job training chefs at a local college. In 1989, she opened a successful restaurant called Napoli. At some point, Power told Duncan who she really was. He agreed to keep her secret.

9   As the years passed, some people forgot about Katherine Ann Power. But to many others, she remained a powerful symbol. To fellow radicals, she was the "one who got away." Said one former protestor, "Kathy Power had become something of a mythic figure. Always out there, always free. The one the police couldn't catch." To the FBI, Power was one of America's Most Wanted criminals,

Fugitive Katherine Ann Power, 44, in court after spending 23 years in hiding

considered armed and very dangerous. To the family of William Schroeder, Power was a cold-blooded killer. "It's always been with us," said one of the nine Schroeder children years after their father was shot. "We think about it every day." And to the Power family back in Denver, Katherine Ann Power was the daughter they had lost, the sweet young girl who had somehow lost her way.

10   Meanwhile, Power herself was wracked by guilt. Outwardly, her life seemed happy enough but privately she was tormented by her past. Every day she woke up with the knowledge that her actions had helped to kill a good, hard-working man who had left behind a grieving family. She thought of her own family, whom she missed terribly but whom she could never again contact. Sometimes depression overtook her. Other times she was paralyzed by the fear that she would slip up and sign her name "Katherine Power" instead of "Alice Metzinger."

11   In 1993, Power decided that enough was enough. She couldn't go on living as Alice Metzinger any longer. She had to face her past, admit her mistakes, and take responsibility for what she had done. She contacted a lawyer and authorized him to begin negotiating with police. By September 1993, a deal had been arranged. She would surrender herself to Boston police. First, though, Power put her affairs in order. She sold her restaurant. She married Ron Duncan and arranged for him to formally adopt her son. Finally, she invited friends to a "farewell party." The invitation didn't reveal much; it simply said she would soon be leaving for "parts unknown."

12   At the party, Power told her friends the shocking truth. Most of them vowed to support her. A few even said they didn't think she should turn herself in. But Power told them she was ready to face "whatever consequences the legal system will impose." Several weeks later, Power learned what those consequences would be. After pleading guilty to armed robbery and manslaughter, she was sentenced to 8 to 12 years in prison, followed by 20 years of probation. Some people were disappointed by the sentence, thinking it was either too little or too much. But Power herself was relieved—relieved that the years of running from the truth were finally over. As she put it, "I am now learning to live with openness and truth, rather than shame and hiddenness." 🍃

If you have been timed while reading this article, enter your reading time below. Then turn to the Words-per-Minute Table on page 195 and look up your reading speed (words per minute). Enter your reading speed on the graph on page 196.

Reading Time: **Lesson 16**

_____ : _____
Minutes   Seconds

A Finding the Main Idea

One statement below expresses the main idea of the article. One statement is too general, or too broad. The other statement explains only part of the article; it is too narrow. Label the statements using the following key:

M—Main Idea **B—Too Broad** **N—Too Narrow**

_____ 1. The war in Vietnam forever changed the lives of many young people, including Katherine Ann Power.

_____ 2. When Katherine Ann Power decided to go into hiding from police, she adopted the name of a dead girl who had been born around the same time as she herself had been born.

_____ 3. Katherine Ann Power, an "all-American girl," became a violent anti-war protester and lived for years in hiding before finally surrendering to the police.

_____ Score 15 points for a correct M answer.

_____ Score 5 points for each correct B or N answer.

_____ **Total Score:** Finding the Main Idea

B Recalling Facts

How well do you remember the facts in the article? Put an X in the box next to the answer that correctly completes each statement about the article.

1. Power planned to use the money she would get from the bank robbery to
   ☐ a. pay her tuition at Brandeis.
   ☐ b. start a new anti-war organization.
   ☐ c. buy weapons.

2. Power's role in the bank robbery was to
   ☐ a. drive the getaway car.
   ☐ b. watch for the arrival of police.
   ☐ c. hold a gun on the bank tellers.

3. In hiding, Power pretended that her name was
   ☐ a. Susan Saxe.
   ☐ b. Alice Metzinger.
   ☐ c. Alice Bond.

4. Power settled down and bought a house in
   ☐ a. Oregon.
   ☐ b. Massachusetts.
   ☐ c. Kentucky.

5. According to the article, Power was found guilty of
   ☐ a. illegal possession of firearms.
   ☐ b. arson and murder.
   ☐ c. armed robbery and manslaughter.

Score 5 points for each correct answer.

_____ **Total Score:** Recalling Facts

C | Making Inferences

When you combine your own experience and information from a text to draw a conclusion that is not directly stated in that text, you are making an inference. Below are five statements that may or may not be inferences based on information in the article. Label the statements using the following key:

C—Correct Inference   F—Faulty Inference

_____ 1. Katherine Ann Power threw herself wholeheartedly into her chosen activities.

_____ 2. When you cross any state line in the U.S., you are required to show proper identification to border guards.

_____ 3. All college students at the time of the Vietnam War were against the war.

_____ 4. If you raise your daughter with love and care, you can be sure that she will never get into trouble with the police.

_____ 5. The police never completely stop looking for suspects they think are responsible for someone's death.

Score 5 points for each correct answer.

_____ **Total Score:** Making Inferences

D | Using Words Precisely

Each numbered sentence below contains an underlined word or phrase from the article. Following the sentence are three definitions. One definition is closest to the meaning of the underlined word. One definition is opposite or nearly opposite. Label those two definitions using the following key. Do not label the remaining definition.

C—Closest   O—Opposite or Nearly Opposite

1. The Vietnam War was <u>escalating</u> and college campuses across the country were becoming hotbeds of anti-war sentiment.

_____ a. morally wrong

_____ b. shrinking

_____ c. expanding

2. At first, she was no more <u>radical</u> than other college students.

_____ a. eager for extreme changes

_____ b. foolish

_____ c. satisfied with things as they are

3. She drifted from city to city, taking <u>menial</u> jobs that required no references.

_____ a. highly respected

_____ b. lowly

_____ c. fascinating

4. For the next 16 years, Power <u>masqueraded as</u> Metzinger.

_____ a. followed

_____ b. disguised herself as

_____ c. truthfully admitted to be

5. Kathy Power had become something of a <u>mythic</u> figure.

_____ a. legendary

_____ b. lost

_____ c. common, everyday

_____ Score 3 points for each correct C answer.

_____ Score 2 points for each correct O answer.

_____ **Total Score:** Using Words Precisely

Enter the four total scores in the spaces below, and add them together to find your Reading Comprehension Score. Then record your score on the graph on page 197.

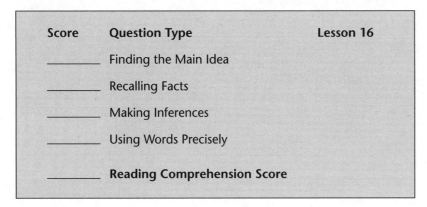

Score	Question Type	Lesson 16
_____	Finding the Main Idea	
_____	Recalling Facts	
_____	Making Inferences	
_____	Using Words Precisely	
_____	**Reading Comprehension Score**	

Author's Approach

Put an X in the box next to the correct answer.

1. The main purpose of the first paragraph is to

☐ a. compare Katherine Ann Power as a teenager and at age 21.

☐ b. emphasize the similarities between Power and other criminals.

☐ c. convey a mood of tension.

2. From the statements below, choose those that you believe the author would agree with.

☐ a. Katherine Ann Power was partly responsible for the death of policeman William Schroeder.

☐ b. Katherine Ann Power became a dangerous criminal during her college years.

☐ c. Katherine Ann Power should not be held responsible for crimes she committed in order to end the war in Vietnam.

3. Choose the statement below that best describes the author's position in paragraph 9.

☐ a. Power stood for different ideas to the various people who knew her or knew about her.

☐ b. Power should be remembered as a symbol of freedom.

☐ c. Power should never be forgiven for her role in William Schroeder's death.

_____ Number of correct answers

Record your personal assessment of your work on the Critical Thinking Chart on page 198.

Summarizing and Paraphrasing

Follow the directions provided for question 1. Put an X in the box next to the correct answer for question 2.

1. Reread paragraph 6 in the article. Below, write a summary of the paragraph in no more than 25 words.

_____

_____

_____

_____

Reread your summary and decide if the summary covers important parts of the paragraph. Next, decide how to shorten the summary to 15 words or less without leaving out any essential information. Write this summary below.

_____

_____

_____

2. Choose the sentence that correctly restates the following sentence from the article:

    "First, though, Power put her affairs in order."

    ☐ a.   First, Power made a list of everything she needed to do.

    ☐ b.   First, Power took care of tasks related to her personal life.

    ☐ c.   First, Power arranged all her crimes in order.

_____ Number of correct answers

Record your personal assessment of your work on the Critical Thinking Chart on page 198.

Critical Thinking

Put an X in the box next to the correct answer for questions 1, 4, and 5. Follow the directions provided for the other questions.

1. From what Power said after she turned herself in to police, you can predict that

    ☐ a.   to protect her family, Power will probably change her name after she is released from prison.

    ☐ b.   she thinks that everyone should tell lies now and then.

    ☐ c.   she will try to tell the truth from now on.

2. Using what you know about Katherine Ann Power and what is told about Susan Saxe in the article, name one way Katherine Ann Power is similar to and one way she is different from Susan Saxe. Cite the paragraph number(s) where you found details in the article to support your conclusions.

    Similarity

_____

_____

    Difference

_____

_____

3. Think about cause-effect relationships in the article. Fill in the blanks in the cause-effect chart, drawing from the letters below.

Cause   Effect

Power was against the Vietnam War.   _____

_____   William Schroeder was killed.

_____   Power finally surrendered to police.

a. Power couldn't stand living a lie anymore.

b. Power became involved in anti-war organizations.

c. Schroeder interrupted a bank robbery.

4. Of the following theme categories, which would this story fit into?

☐ a. Extreme actions in defense of what you believe are never crimes.

☐ b. Blood is thicker than water.

☐ c. The truth will set you free.

5. What did you have to do to answer question 2?

☐ a. find an opinion (what someone thinks about something)

☐ b. find a summary (synthesized information)

☐ c. find a comparison (how things are the same)

_____ Number of correct answers

Record your personal assessment of your work on the Critical Thinking Chart on page 198.

Personal Response

Would you recommend this article to other students? Explain.

_____

_____

_____

_____

_____

Self-Assessment

I can't really understand how

_____

_____

_____

_____

CRITICAL THINKING

QUIZ SHOW FIX

Charles Van Doren fidgeted in his isolation booth on the set of NBC's TV quiz show *Twenty-One*. Somehow he had to come up with the answer to a question about a character who sings a certain song in an Italian opera. The game was on the line. Van Doren's brow wrinkled and his breathing grew heavier as the clock ticked down to the final second. Millions of viewers could see him sweat and hear him whispering softly to himself. "She sings it right at the end of a party given by… What's her name!" he mumbled. "Her name is like…Violetta. Violetta!"

2   That was the correct answer, so Van Doren won the game, along with thousands of dollars in prize money. But he needn't have sweated; he knew the answer all along. The producers of *Twenty-One* had given it to him before the show began. In truth, they provided Van Doren with every answer to every question. His facial grimaces, his hesitation, and his last-second blurting out of the right answer were all part of an elaborate act. Although no one in the TV audience suspected it at the time, the quiz show was fixed.

"Twenty-One" quiz show host Jack Barry at the final telecasting of the show on October 16, 1958

3   *Twenty-One* was only one of many quiz shows that gripped the nation in the late 1950s. Others included *Tic-Tac-Dough, The Big Surprise,* and *Do You Trust Your Wife?* Quiz show mania began on June 7, 1955. That was when *The $64,000 Question* made its TV debut on CBS. The show was an instant sensation, winning millions of viewers. No other program in history had ever achieved such a huge audience so fast.

4   NBC didn't want to be left out in the cold, so it developed a quiz show of its own called *Twenty-One.* The show's concept was based on the card game known as *twenty-one* or *blackjack.* The winner was the player whose score reached or came the closest to the number *21.* The questions were ranked by difficulty ranging from one to 11. Contestants accumulated points and money for each correct answer. The show made its first appearance on September 12, 1956.

5   At first *Twenty-One* was a dud. The questions, which ranged over 108 topics, were simply too difficult, so that the score at the end of the show was often zero to zero. The audience was disappointed; it wanted to see people win and win big. Then the show's producer, Daniel Enright, found the answer to his prayers in the form of a man named Herbert Stempel.

Stempel was a U.S. Army veteran and student at New York City College. He was, to use Stempel's own words, a "little, short, squat guy," but he was also extremely smart and possessed a terrific memory.

6   Enright wanted to promote Stempel as "the common man" who happened to be a genius. Here was someone, thought Enright, who would appeal to the audience. So Enright instructed Stempel to dress for the role—a shirt with a frayed collar, a poorly-fitted suit, and an ugly haircut. Enright also coached Stempel to stutter, to bite his lips, and to wipe his brow before answering difficult questions. And, to make sure his plan was successful, Enright gave Stempel all the answers to the questions he would be asked.

7   Stempel, of course, easily romped over his opponents. In the span of eight weeks he won every contest, raking in $69,500 in total winnings. Stempel, who had started out poor, was now a fairly wealthy man. Equally important to him, he had become a celebrity. Strangers stopped him on the street and asked for his autograph. Meanwhile, *Twenty-One* became a smash hit as its ratings skyrocketed.

8   Although Stempel didn't realize it, by November his time in the spotlight was coming to an end. Enright had found someone else who he believed would be

even more popular with audiences. This man's name was Charles Van Doren, son of the famous poet Mark Van Doren. Charles Van Doren was the polar opposite of Herbert Stempel. He was tall, good-looking, well-dressed, and well-educated. He was also a teacher at Columbia University.

9   Just before the show on November 28, 1956, Enright broke the news to Stempel: he was being pushed out, the show needed a new champ. Stempel was

Charles Van Doren as a contestant on "Twenty-One"

devastated. He thought he could beat Van Doren in a fair match, but Enright didn't give him that chance. Stempel was ordered to miss a question.

10   And so that night, Stempel and Van Doren each stepped into their separate isolation booths so they couldn't hear any answers shouted from the live studio audience. Stempel was asked to name the movie that won the 1955 Oscar for Best Picture. Ironically, the Oscar-winner happened to be *Marty*, his favorite movie. But this was the question he had been told to miss, and so he deliberately gave a wrong answer.

11   The nation hailed the new *Twenty-One* champion. Van Doren quickly became the most popular and most talked-about person on TV. Thousands of fan letters and job offers poured in every week. Van Doren was a hero to school teachers because he made being smart seem so cool. He was also a hero to parents who thought he was a better idol for their children than rock singer Elvis Presley.

12   Van Doren reigned as the champion of *Twenty-One* until March 11, 1957. Then he lost in a prearranged match with a woman lawyer. During that time he had amassed $129,000 in winnings—a staggering sum in those days. It was, said Van Doren, "more money than I had ever made or ever dreamed of making."

13   Meanwhile, an envious and severely depressed Stempel had been stewing over his rigged defeat. He wanted everyone to know the truth about the show, so he began telling his story around town. At first, no one paid any attention to him, dismissing him as a sore loser. But then others, too, claimed that quiz shows were fixed. Finally, a New York district attorney named Frank Hogan decided to investigate all the quiz shows. He discovered that almost all of them were rigged.

14   Everyone connected with *Twenty-One* denied the charges. Van Doren told reporters that "at no time was I coached or tutored."

15   But the lies couldn't hold up when the U.S. Congress started its own investigation. It called Charles Van Doren to testify. His first response was to withdraw from the public eye, which he did for a few days. But there was no place for him to hide. "I simply ran away. There were a dozen newsmen outside my door and I was running from them, too," he later explained. "I could not bear to have my family, my friends, and the general public know I had deceived them."

16   At last, on November 2, 1959, Charles Van Doren came clean. In his speech before Congress, which lasted more than an hour and a half, he traced step-by-step his own involvement in the sordid mess. Van Doren confessed everything, including his own lies to cover up the scandal. He appeared to be genuinely sorry for his role in the affair. "I would give almost anything I have to reverse the course of my life in the last three years."

17   Amazingly, no one went to jail—despite the fact that at least 100 witnesses had committed perjury. But one man paid a high price for his part in the scandal. That man was Charles Van Doren. Columbia University fired him right after his speech to Congress. The next day, NBC also let him go from a $50,000-a-year job it had given him. Worst of all, his personal reputation was forever tarnished.

If you have been timed while reading this article, enter your reading time below. Then turn to the Words-per-Minute Table on page 195 and look up your reading speed (words per minute). Enter your reading speed on the graph on page 196.

Reading Time: **Lesson 17**

_____ : _____
Minutes   Seconds

A | Finding the Main Idea

One statement below expresses the main idea of the article. One statement is too general, or too broad. The other statement explains only part of the article; it is too narrow. Label the statements using the following key:

M—Main Idea   **B—Too Broad**   **N—Too Narrow**

_____ 1. Contestants on a 1950s quiz show called *Twenty-One* were given all the answers before the show; eventually the deception was uncovered and the contestants were disgraced.

_____ 2. When Herbert Stempel repeatedly outanswered his opponents on the quiz show *Twenty-One*, he became a national celebrity.

_____ 3. The quiz shows we see on TV are not always what they seem to be, as proven by the 1950s quiz show *Twenty-One*.

_____ Score 15 points for a correct M answer.

_____ Score 5 points for each correct B or N answer.

_____ **Total Score:** Finding the Main Idea

B | Recalling Facts

How well do you remember the facts in the article? Put an X in the box next to the answer that correctly completes each statement about the article.

1. Besides *Twenty-One*, another TV quiz show mentioned in this article is
   ☐ a. *The $64,000 Question.*
   ☐ b. *Get Smart.*
   ☐ c. *To Tell the Truth.*

2. At first, *Twenty-One* was not popular because the
   ☐ a. contestants were too smart.
   ☐ b. questions were too difficult.
   ☐ c. show's host was annoying.

3. Charles Van Doren was a
   ☐ a. famous poet.
   ☐ b. student at New York City College.
   ☐ c. teacher at Columbia University.

4. *Twenty-One* fooled the public by
   ☐ a. controlling which contestant would win.
   ☐ b. using actors instead of real contestants.
   ☐ c. not really awarding the money they claimed they gave out.

5. Herbert Stempel was forced to answer this question wrong so Charles Van Doren could win the game:
   ☐ a. Who is Elvis Presley?
   ☐ b. Which character sings a famous song in a certain opera?
   ☐ c. Which movie won the 1955 Oscar for Best Picture?

Score 5 points for each correct answer.

_____ **Total Score:** Recalling Facts

C Making Inferences

When you combine your own experience and information from a text to draw a conclusion that is not directly stated in that text, you are making an inference. Below are five statements that may or may not be inferences based on information in the article. Label the statements using the following key:

C—Correct Inference   **F—Faulty Inference**

_____ 1. The American public demands that its celebrities be good looking and well dressed.

_____ 2. Audiences are more likely to believe in a contestant who has trouble answering a question than one who knows the answer right away.

_____ 3. The lure of easy money often makes people do things for which they are later ashamed.

_____ 4. Whenever anyone on the TV tells a lie, the U.S. Congress begins an investigation.

_____ 5. Universities such as Columbia demand honesty and respectability from their teachers.

Score 5 points for each correct answer.

_____ **Total Score:** Making Inferences

D Using Words Precisely

Each numbered sentence below contains an underlined word or phrase from the article. Following the sentence are three definitions. One definition is closest to the meaning of the underlined word. One definition is opposite or nearly opposite. Label those two definitions using the following key. Do not label the remaining definition.

C—Closest   **O—Opposite or Nearly Opposite**

1. Stempel was <u>devastated</u>.

_____ a. overwhelmed by grief or anger

_____ b. important

_____ c. filled with happiness

2. During that time he had <u>amassed</u> $129,000 in winnings—a staggering sum in those days.

_____ a. needed

_____ b. collected

_____ c. distributed

3. During that time he had amassed $129,000 in winnings —a <u>staggering</u> sum in those days.

_____ a. normal

_____ b. astonishing

_____ c. disgusting

4. In his speech before Congress, which lasted more than an hour and a half, he traced step-by-step his own involvement in the <u>sordid</u> mess.

_____ a. strange

_____ b. respectable

_____ c. shameful

5. Worst of all, his personal reputation was forever <u>tarnished</u>.

_____ a. stained

_____ b. kept in perfect condition

_____ c. remembered

_____ Score 3 points for each correct C answer.

_____ Score 2 points for each correct O answer.

_____ **Total Score:** Using Words Precisely

Enter the four total scores in the spaces below, and add them together to find your Reading Comprehension Score. Then record your score on the graph on page 197.

Score	Question Type	Lesson 17
_____	Finding the Main Idea	
_____	Recalling Facts	
_____	Making Inferences	
_____	Using Words Precisely	
_____	**Reading Comprehension Score**	

Author's Approach

Put an X in the box next to the correct answer.

1. What does the author mean by the statement "the quiz show was fixed"?
☐ a. The show was always aired at the same time each week.
☐ b. The show had been changed to make it more attractive to audiences.
☐ c. The show was controlled in a dishonest way.

2. The main purpose of the first paragraph is to
☐ a. explain how the quiz show *Twenty-One* came to be dishonest.
☐ b. describe the scene on a typical *Twenty-One* quiz show.
☐ c. express an opinion about quiz shows

3. Judging by statements from the article "Quiz Show Fix," you can conclude that the author wants the reader to think that Charles Van Doren was
☐ a. not as smart as Herbert Stempel.
☐ b. a bitter and depressed person.
☐ c. basically a good man who made a big mistake.

4. The author tells this story mainly by
☐ a. using his or her imagination and creativity.
☐ c. explaining complex ideas in a logical order.
☐ c. describing a series of events related to the same topic.

_____ Number of correct answers

Record your personal assessment of your work on the Critical Thinking Chart on page 198.

CRITICAL THINKING

Summarizing and Paraphrasing

Follow the directions provided for question 1. Put an X in the box next to the correct answer for the other questions.

1. Reread paragraph 7 in the article. Below, write a summary of the paragraph in no more than 25 words.

_____

_____

_____

Reread your summary and decide whether it covers the important ideas in the paragraph. Next, try to shorten the summary to 15 words or less without leaving out any essential information. Write this summary below.

_____

_____

_____

2. Read the statement about the article below. Then read the paraphrase of that statement. Choose the reason that best tells why the paraphrase does not say the same thing as the statement.

Statement: Angry and depressed, Stempel began to tell the truth about the quiz show.

Paraphrase: Feeling angry and depressed, Stempel wanted everyone in town to know how dishonest the show was, but, at first, few people believed him.

☐ a. Paraphrase says too much.

☐ b. Paraphrase doesn't say enough.

☐ c. Paraphrase doesn't agree with the statement about the article.

3. Choose the best one-sentence paraphrase for the following sentence from the article:

"At last, on November 2, 1959, Charles Van Doren came clean."

☐ a. Finally, on November 2, 1959, Charles Van Doren admitted to his dishonest activities.

☐ b. Finally, on November 2, 1959, Charles Van Doren testified before Congress, dressed in a clean suit.

☐ c. Finally, on November 2, 1959, Charles Van Doren began to talk to reporters outside his home.

_____ Number of correct answers

Record your personal assessment of your work on the Critical Thinking Chart on page 198.

Critical Thinking

Put an X in the box next to the correct answer for questions 1 and 5. Follow the directions provided for the other questions.

1. Judging by what you learned about Charles Van Doren from the article, you can predict that if he were asked to be part of another deception, he would

☐ a. consider the offer seriously.

☐ b. try another deception to see if he could make more money.

☐ c. refuse the offer.

2. Using what you know about Herbert Stempel and what is told about Charles Van Doren in the article, name three ways Herbert Stempel is similar to and three ways Herbert Stempel is different from Charles Van Doren. Cite the paragraph number(s) where you found details in the article to support your conclusions.

Similarities

_____

_____

_____

Differences

_____

_____

_____

3. Choose from the letters below to correctly complete the following statement. Write the letters on the lines.

   On the positive side, _____, but on the negative side _____.

   a. Charles Van Doren ruined his reputation on the quiz show

   b. Charles Van Doren was the son of a poet

   c. Charles Van Doren made a lot of money

4. Read paragraph 13. Then choose from the letters below to correctly complete the following statement. Write the letters on the lines.

   According to paragraph 13, _____ happened because _____.

   a. Herbert Stempel began to spread the word that the show was fixed

   b. Almost all the quiz shows were rigged

   c. Herbert Stempel was angry about the way he had been treated by the quiz show's producer

5. What did you have to do to answer question 1?

   ☐ a. find a fact (something that you can prove is true)

   ☐ b. find a question (something that is asked)

   ☐ c. make a prediction (guess what might happen in the future based on clues)

_____ Number of correct answers

Record your personal assessment of your work on the Critical Thinking Chart on page 74.

Personal Response

Why do you think Charles Van Doren agreed to be part of the *Twenty-One* deception?

_____

_____

_____

_____

Self-Assessment

When reading the article, I was having trouble with

_____

_____

_____

_____

CRITICAL THINKING

MATA HARI
From Footlights to Firing Squad

French soldiers at the World War I Battle of Verdun in 1916

Her name—Mata Hari—has a mysterious and exotic ring to it. Even today it conjures up an image of intrigue and espionage. The name fit the woman perfectly. Mata Hari lived her life on the edge, at times taking enormous risks. In the end, she paid for her daring before a French firing squad.

2   Mata Hari was the stage name of Margaretha Geertruida Zelle. She was born in Holland on August 7, 1876. She had black hair, brown eyes, and an olive complexion. These physical features would later play a key role in her life, allowing her to claim she was half Indian.

3   When Margaretha was 15, her mother died. Her father then sent her away to live with her godfather. By age 18, Margaretha was restless with life in Holland. One day she saw an advertisement in the newspaper. It read, "Captain in the Army of the Indies, on leave in Holland, seeks wife." Three months after meeting Captain Rudolf MacLeod, Margaretha married him. They went to live in the Dutch East Indies (now Indonesia). Life with the captain, however, was extremely unpleasant. The couple separated in 1902 and divorced four years later.

4   Suddenly on her own, Margaretha went to Paris to live. While there, she decided to become a "Hindu" dancer. In the Dutch East Indies, she had seen many native dances and had learned enough about dancers to pass herself off as one. She selected a new name for herself: Mata Hari, meaning "the light of day." As time went by, she invented a whole new history of her life. For example, Margaretha told people she descended from a royal Asian family and had been a "sacred" dancer in a Ganges temple.

5   Mata Hari wasn't a brilliant dancer, but she was a big hit anyway. This was due more to her scanty costumes than to her art. Mata Hari often performed in little more than a few wispy veils. This was an integral part of her temple ritual, she claimed. To audiences at the time it was a novelty, a bit shocking—but thrilling, too. Between 1905 and 1914, she drew enthusiastic crowds in cities such as Paris, Milan, and Madrid.

6   Meanwhile, famous and powerful men were flocking to her side. They included artists, bankers, diplomats, and members of royal families. These men showered her with money and gifts. Mata Hari basked in her fame and the luxury it brought.

7   In May 1914, Mata Hari went to Germany to dance. She was there when World War I broke out in August. She attempted to go back to France, now Germany's enemy, but the Germans confiscated her money, furs, and jewelry. Nearly broke, she suddenly had no choice but to return to her native Holland.

8   By that time, 38-year-old Mata Hari's dancing days were over. Still, she had assets. She was intelligent, spoke several languages fluently, and had close contacts with people in high places on both sides of the war. She seemed ideally suited to be a spy. Both the French and the Germans tried to recruit her.

9   In May 1916, the Germans paid her 20,000 francs to spy for them, even assigning her the code name of "H21." Foolishly, she took the money even though she later claimed she had no intention of working for them. To her, it was compensation for what the Germans had stolen from her back in 1914. Later that year, Mata Hari agreed to spy for the French. Again, money was the key factor: the French promised to pay her well.

10   The French sent Mata Hari to Spain to spy on the Germans there. In Spain, she connected with a German major named Arnold Kalle, who apparently figured out Mata Hari's scheme to double-cross the Germans. He pretended to trust her, however, feeding her a mixture of lies and unimportant truths.

11   Meanwhile, Kalle and his bosses plotted to destroy Mata Hari. They were

Mata Hari dressed for dancing. Whom did she really spy for—Germany or France?

angry with her for taking their money and then spying for the French. They sent a series of coded messages to and from Berlin, all about agent H21. The Germans used an old code they knew the French had broken. In other words, they wanted the French to read these messages.

12 The French took the bait. When they decoded the messages, they concluded that Mata Hari was actually working for the Germans. On February 13, 1917, they arrested her for espionage.

13 This was a trying time for the French. The war was not going well. They were losing battles and French soldiers were dying in record numbers. It was easy for the government to shift blame from itself to "foreign spies." Before the war was over, the French would execute nearly 300 people for spying.

14 The police questioned Mata Hari day and night. Not surprisingly, they caught her in many petty lies. After all, Mata Hari had fabricated so much of her past that it was difficult even for her to separate fact from fiction. The police used her confusion to prove she was a born liar.

15 At her trial, the prosecutor reminded the jury of the thousands of soldiers dying on the battlefields. He left no question as to who was responsible. Brave French soldiers were being betrayed by spies like Mata Hari. "The evil that this woman has done is unbelievable," he declared. "This is perhaps the greatest woman spy of the century."

16 It took the jury only 40 minutes to return a verdict of guilty. Mata Hari had protested her innocence from the beginning, but after the trial, she became philosophical. "I am a woman who enjoys herself very much," she wrote from her prison cell. "Sometimes I lose, sometimes I win."

17 Mata Hari was also courageous. On October 15, 1917, she fixed her hair and picked out the clothes for her execution. She wanted to go out with style. When a soldier started to tie her wrists to the stake, she said, "That will not be necessary." She also refused a blindfold. One of the soldiers muttered, "This lady knows how to die."

18 When the commanding officer raised his sword, Mata Hari said, "Thank you, sir." She then lifted her hands and blew a kiss to the firing squad. As the commanding officer dropped his sword, Mata Hari turned her head slightly and smiled.

19 Whose side was Mata Hari really on? We may never know for sure. Most of the court records have been destroyed. In any case, as a spy, she wasn't very good. The information passed on by "the greatest woman spy of the century" had no value to either side.

If you have been timed while reading this article, enter your reading time below. Then turn to the Words-per-Minute Table on page 195 and look up your reading speed (words per minute). Enter your reading speed on the graph on page 196.

Reading Time: Lesson 19

_____ : _____
Minutes   Seconds

A | Finding the Main Idea

One statement below expresses the main idea of the article. One statement is too general, or too broad. The other statement explains only part of the article; it is too narrow. Label the statements using the following key:

M—Main Idea   **B—Too Broad**   **N—Too Narrow**

_____ 1. Claiming to have been a dancer in a Hindu temple, Mata Hari became the toast of Europe, performing in all the major cities.

_____ 2. Mata Hari's habits of bending the truth and living on the edge helped her gain fame as a dancer but also led to her conviction as a spy and her death by firing squad.

_____ 3. Mata Hari first became famous as an entertainer, but unfortunately her name was soon linked to sadness and death.

_____ Score 15 points for a correct M answer.

_____ Score 5 points for each correct B or N answer.

_____ **Total Score:** Finding the Main Idea

B | Recalling Facts

How well do you remember the facts in the article? Put an X in the box next to the answer that correctly completes each statement about the article.

1. Mata Hari was born in
☐ a. Holland.
☐ b. India.
☐ c. Indonesia.

2. According to the article, Mata Hari's dances were popular mostly because she performed them
☐ a. accompanied by authentic Indian music.
☐ b. for free.
☐ c. wearing just a few wispy veils.

3. Mata Hari said that she agreed to be a spy for Germany because she
☐ a. believed in the German cause.
☐ b. thought they owed her money for taking her possessions.
☐ c. was afraid that they would kill her if she refused.

4. On February 13, 1917, Mata Hari was arrested for espionage by
☐ a. Germany.
☐ b. France.
☐ c. Holland.

5. At her execution, Mata Hari acted
☐ a. haughty and angry.
☐ b. frantic and out of control.
☐ c. calm and courageous.

Score 5 points for each correct answer.

_____ **Total Score:** Recalling Facts

C | Making Inferences

When you combine your own experience and information from a text to draw a conclusion that is not directly stated in that text, you are making an inference. Below are five statements that may or may not be inferences based on information in the article. Label the statements using the following key:

C—Correct Inference   **F—Faulty Inference**

_____ 1. Mata Hari did not believe she was putting herself in danger when she accepted money from the Germans.

_____ 2. It was fairly easy to travel around Europe at the beginning of the twentieth century.

_____ 3. During World War I, all spies underwent special training.

_____ 4. According to Mata Hari's personal code of behavior, it was all right to tell lies.

_____ 5. Audiences in Europe were quite familiar with Hindu dances during the early part of the twentieth century.

Score 5 points for each correct answer.

_____ **Total Score:** Making Inferences

D | Using Words Precisely

Each numbered sentence below contains an underlined word or phrase from the article. Following the sentence are three definitions. One definition is closest to the meaning of the underlined word. One definition is opposite or nearly opposite. Label those two definitions using the following key. Do not label the remaining definition.

C—Closest   O—Opposite or Nearly Opposite

1. This was an <u>integral</u> part of her temple ritual, she claimed.

_____ a. unnecessary

_____ b. essential

_____ c. ancient

2. To audiences at the time it was a <u>novelty</u>, a bit shocking—but thrilling, too.

_____ a. something new or unusual

_____ b. something disgusting

_____ c. something common and ordinary

3. She attempted to go back to France,…but the Germans <u>confiscated</u> her money, furs, and jewelry.

_____ a. returned

_____ b. destroyed

_____ c. seized

4. After all, Mata Hari had <u>fabricated</u> so much of her past that it was difficult even for her to separate fact from fiction.

_____ a. forgotten

_____ b. made up

_____ c. reported accurately

5. Mata Hari had protested her innocence from the beginning, but after the trial, she became <u>philosophical</u>.

_____ a. frantic

_____ b. confused

_____ c. untroubled when facing danger or disaster

_____ Score 3 points for each correct C answer.

_____ Score 2 points for each correct O answer.

_____ **Total Score:** Using Words Precisely

Enter the four total scores in the spaces below, and add them together to find your Reading Comprehension Score. Then record your score on the graph on page 197.

Score	Question Type	Lesson 18
_____	Finding the Main Idea	
_____	Recalling Facts	
_____	Making Inferences	
_____	Using Words Precisely	
_____	**Reading Comprehension Score**	

Author's Approach

Put an X in the box next to the correct answer.

1. What is the author's purpose in writing "Mata Hari: From Footlights to Firing Squad"?

☐ a. To persuade the reader to tell the truth at all times

☐ b. To inform the reader about an interesting person

☐ c. To express an opinion about war

2. Which of the following statements from the article best describes Mata Hari's physical appearance?

☐ a. "She was intelligent, spoke several languages fluently, and had close contacts with people in high places on both sides of the war."

☐ b. "Mata Hari was also courageous."

☐ c. "She had black hair, brown eyes, and an olive complexion."

3. In this article, "Meanwhile, famous and powerful men were flocking to her side" means that Mata Hari was

☐ a. popular with many men.

☐ b. never alone; men accompanied her everywhere she went.

☐ c. often joined by men in her dance performances.

4. What does the author imply by saying "The information passed on by 'the greatest woman spy of the century' had no value to either side"?

☐ a. Neither Germany nor France ever really trusted Mata Hari.

☐ b. Mata Hari deserved to die because she had not done her job well.

☐ c. Mata Hari did not deserve her reputation.

_____ Number of correct answers

Record your personal assessment of your work on the Critical Thinking Chart on page 198.

CRITICAL THINKING

Summarizing and Paraphrasing

Follow the directions provided for the other question 1. Put an X in the box next to the correct answer for the other questions.

1. Complete the following one-sentence summary of the article using the lettered phrases from the phrase bank below. Write the letters on the lines.

> **Phrase Bank:**
>
> a. a description of her early life
>
> b. how she gained fame and put herself in danger
>
> c. information about her trial and execution

The article about Mata Hari begins with _____, goes on to explain _____, and ends with _____.

2. Below are summaries of the article. Choose the summary that says all the most important things about the article but in the fewest words.

- ☐ a. Mata Hari was a famous dancer in Europe who was accused of being a spy during World War I and was executed by France in 1917.

- ☐ b. Even though Mata Hari was executed by a firing squad, she maintained until her death that she was innocent.

- ☐ c. Although Mata Hari had been born in Holland, she claimed to have descended from a royal Asian family and to have been a "sacred" dancer in a temple; even though she said that she was not a spy, she was executed for espionage by France during World War I.

3. Choose the best one-sentence paraphrase for the following sentence from the article:

"This was a trying time for the French."

- ☐ a. At this time, the French were trying to time events.

- ☐ b. The French were trying hard to succeed at this point.

- ☐ c. At this time, things were not going well for the French.

_____ Number of correct answers

Record your personal assessment of your work on the Critical Thinking Chart on page 198.

Critical Thinking

Follow the directions provided for the other questions 1, 2, and 3. Put an X in the box next to the correct answer for the other questions.

1. For each statement below, write O if it expresses an opinion or write F if it expresses a fact.

_____ a. Her name—Mata Hari—has a mysterious and exotic ring to it.

_____ b. In any case, as a spy, she wasn't very good.

_____ c. Between 1905 and 1914, she drew enthusiastic crowds in cities such as Paris, Milan, and Madrid.

2. Choose from the letters below to correctly complete the following statement. Write the letters on the lines.

On the positive side, _____, but on the negative side _____.

a. Mata Hari lived life fully and freely

b. Mata Hari's way of living put her in great danger

c. Mata Hari was eager to make money

3. Read paragraph 11. Then choose from the letters below to correctly complete the following statement. Write the letters on the lines.

    According to paragraph 11, _____ happened because _____.

    a. Mata Hari had taken German money but was spying for the French

    b. the Germans knew that their code had been broken

    c. the German officer, Major Kalle, tried to destroy Mata Hari

4. What was the cause of France's conclusion that Mata Hari was a spy for the Germans?

    ☐ a. Mata Hari seemed to like Germany better than France.

    ☐ b. The French were doing badly in battles.

    ☐ c. The French were deceived by fake messages sent by the Germans.

5. What did you have to do to answer question 3?

    ☐ a. find a question (something that is asked)

    ☐ b. find a list (a number of things)

    ☐ c. find an effect (something that happened as a result of another event)

    _____ Number of correct answers

    Record your personal assessment of your work on the Critical Thinking Chart on page 198.

Personal Response

How do you think Mata Hari felt when her mother died and she was sent to live with her godfather?

_____

_____

_____

_____

Self-Assessment

The part I found most difficult about the article was

_____

_____

_____

_____

I found this difficult because

_____

_____

_____

_____

CRITICAL THINKING

THE TUSKEGEE EXPERIMENT

On May 16, 1997, President Bill Clinton issued an official apology. He directed it to a group of African-American men and their families. "No power on Earth can give you back the lives lost, the pain suffered, the years of internal torment and anguish," said Clinton. "What was done cannot be undone. But we can end the silence.... We can look you in the eye and finally say on behalf of the American people, what the United States government did was shameful, and I am sorry."

2   What did the government do that was so awful? The sad story began many years ago in Tuskegee, Alabama. In 1930, this small rural town had the only African-American hospital in the South. Syphilis, a potentially deadly disease, was sweeping through black communities there. Syphilis attacks the central nervous system. It can cause victims to go blind or deaf, or to lose their sanity. It can deform the bones and teeth. Sometimes it attacks the heart. U.S. Public Health officials were alarmed by the growing rate of syphilis among African Americans in the South. To help

President Clinton with Tuskegee survivor Hermon Shaw at the national apology to the survivors and their families.

stop the epidemic, they sent doctors to Tuskegee to treat the victims.

3   But this was the time of the Great Depression. Money was scarce. Funds for the treatment program began to dry up. Then, in 1932, the focus of the Tuskegee program changed. U.S. health officials decided to see how syphilis destroyed the human body by withholding treatment from African-American men. This secret study was called "The Tuskegee Study of Untreated Syphilis in the Negro Male."

4   It was a despicable plan. The fact was that doctors knew how devastating the disease could be if left untreated. A 20-year study on syphilis had already been done in Oslo, Norway. But the 1930s was a time of rampant racism in the United States. Many people in this country believed that blacks were biologically inferior to whites. The Oslo study had been done just with whites; doctors wondered if syphilis might affect blacks differently. Some African-American doctors and nurses went along with the study. They thought the results would show no difference between blacks and whites. In that case, they reasoned, the study would dispel the notion of African-American inferiority.

5   The study began with a massive effort to recruit African-American subjects in Tuskegee and the surrounding region. U.S. Public Health officials talked to African-American men in churches, stores, and private homes. The recruiters did not mention that they were looking for men with syphilis. In fact, they never mentioned syphilis at all. Nor did they tell the men that the study was part of an experiment to test the theory of black inferiority. Instead the recruiters simply said they were selecting men for free medical check-ups.

6   These were hard times in rural Alabama. No one had much money. The recruiters made promises that were hard to resist. In addition to free medical care, they offered free hot lunches and free burial service. As a result, hundreds of African-American men, most with little or no schooling, volunteered for the study.

7   About 400 African-American men with syphilis were chosen to take part in the Tuskegee experiment. Another 200 African-American men without syphilis were picked to serve as a control group so comparisons could be made. The infected men were never told of their condition. They were simply used as human guinea pigs.

8   Looking back, many people believe that one of the worst aspects of the study was how happy the officials made the men feel. The men would be picked up in a fancy government station wagon for their check-ups. One African-American nurse, Eunice Rivers, later wrote, "[It] was a mark of distinction for many of the men who enjoyed waving to their neighbors as they drove by." Rivers added, "They looked forward happily to having the government doctor take their blood pressure and listen to their hearts."

9   But the tragic truth was that the disease was slowly killing many of these

President Clinton apologizes to survivors of the Tuskegee experiment.

men. Twenty-eight men, and perhaps as many as 100 more, died directly as a result of not getting treatment. And 154 more died from the hideous side effects of syphilis.

10   When the Tuskegee study began, there were several treatments for syphilis. None worked well. Most often, chemicals were injected into the victim to slow the progression of the disease. Then, in 1943, the "wonder drug" penicillin was shown to cure syphilis. Within four years, it had become the number one weapon in the fight against syphilis. Just about every doctor in the country was using penicillin to cure syphilis patients. There was only one major exception to the rule—the researchers who were working with the African-American men of Tuskegee. The Public Health doctors refused to give these men the new drug. In short, the men in the Tuskegee experiment were condemned to die in the name of science.

11   And that was the way it remained for more than 25 years, until a newspaper reporter named Jean Heller got wind of the scandal. She spent three weeks doing research. Then, on July 25, 1972, she filed her story. Her grim account of the Tuskegee experiment shocked and outraged many people. A government panel was quickly set up to look into the study. As a result of this probe, the Tuskegee study was shut down. But by 1972, those African-American men still living had suffered 40 years of deliberate medical abuse.

12   In 1973, the NAACP filed a class action suit against the U.S. government on behalf of the survivors. The victims and their families settled for $9 million. The following year, the U.S. government developed new rules governing research conduct. The Tuskegee experiment, with its human guinea pigs, will never be repeated.

13   Still, the bitter memories lingered among the families of the victims. Albert Julkes, Jr., the son of one of the participants, believes that the Tuskegee experiment was "one of the worst atrocities" ever committed by the U.S. government. Says Julkes, "You don't treat dogs that way."

If you have been timed while reading this article, enter your reading time below. Then turn to the Words-per-Minute Table on page 195 and look up your reading speed (words per minute). Enter your reading speed on the graph on page 196.

Reading Time: Lesson 19

_____ : _____
Minutes   Seconds

A | Finding the Main Idea

One statement below expresses the main idea of the article. One statement is too general, or too broad. The other statement explains only part of the article; it is too narrow. Label the statements using the following key:

M—Main Idea   **B—Too Broad**   **N—Too Narrow**

_____ 1. The African-American subjects of the Tuskegee Experiment were not informed that some of them had syphilis, a terrible disease.

_____ 2. It is no wonder that some people are suspicious of the motives of scientists, in light of the horrors of the Tuskegee Experiment.

_____ 3. As part of the shameful Tuskegee Experiment, treatment was withheld from African-American men with syphilis, all in the name of research.

_____ Score 15 points for a correct M answer.

_____ Score 5 points for each correct B or N answer.

_____ **Total Score:** Finding the Main Idea

B | Recalling Facts

How well do you remember the facts in the article? Put an X in the box next to the answer that correctly completes each statement about the article.

1. The Tuskegee Experiment studied the effects of syphilis among
   ☐ a. African-American women.
   ☐ b. African-American men.
   ☐ c. Southern white men.

2. Recruiters told volunteer subjects that they were signing up for
   ☐ a. free medical examinations.
   ☐ b. an experiment involving a serious disease.
   ☐ c. an experiment to test whether blacks were biologically inferior to whites.

3. In 1943, researchers found a drug that could successfully treat syphilis called
   ☐ a. quinine.
   ☐ b. aspirin.
   ☐ c. penicillin.

4. The Tuskegee Experiment was finally brought to the public's attention by
   ☐ a. a newspaper reporter.
   ☐ b. a doctor who had worked in the project.
   ☐ c. one of the research subjects.

5. The victims of the experiment were awarded this amount by the U.S. government:
   ☐ a. $110 million.
   ☐ b. $200 million.
   ☐ c. $9 million.

Score 5 points for each correct answer.

_____ **Total Score:** Recalling Facts

C | Making Inferences

When you combine your own experience and information from a text to draw a conclusion that is not directly stated in that text, you are making an inference. Below are five statements that may or may not be inferences based on information in the article. Label the statements using the following key:

C—Correct Inference   F—Faulty Inference

_____ 1. The discovery of penicillin has wiped out syphilis completely.

_____ 2. The general public of the United States knew nothing about the Tuskegee Experiment until 1972.

_____ 3. Most likely, the researchers who worked on the Tuskegee Experiment did not want anyone to know about their work.

_____ 4. In times when funds are scarce, scientists can still count on the U.S. government to give them all the money they want for research.

_____ 5. Citizens want their governments to follow an honorable code of conduct.

Score 5 points for each correct answer.

_____ **Total Score:** Making Inferences

D | Using Words Precisely

Each numbered sentence below contains an underlined word or phrase from the article. Following the sentence are three definitions. One definition is closest to the meaning of the underlined word. One definition is opposite or nearly opposite. Label those two definitions using the following key. Do not label the remaining definition.

C—Closest   O—Opposite or Nearly Opposite

1. It was a <u>despicable</u> plan.

_____ a. confusing

_____ b. disgraceful

_____ c. honorable

2. But the 1930s was a time of <u>rampant</u> racism in the United States.

_____ a. unchecked

_____ b. dangerous

_____ c. controlled

3. Many people in this country believed that blacks were biologically <u>inferior to</u> whites.

_____ a. better than

_____ b. different from

_____ c. of lower quality than

4. In that case, they reasoned, the study would <u>dispel</u> the notion of African-American inferiority.

_____ a. examine

_____ b. drive away or eliminate

_____ c. prove beyond doubt

5. But by 1972, those African-American men still living had suffered 40 years of <u>deliberate</u> medical abuse.

_____ a. done on purpose

_____ b. cruel

_____ c. accidental

_____ Score 3 points for each correct C answer.

_____ Score 2 points for each correct O answer.

_____ **Total Score:** Using Words Precisely

Enter the four total scores in the spaces below, and add them together to find your Reading Comprehension Score. Then record your score on the graph on page 197.

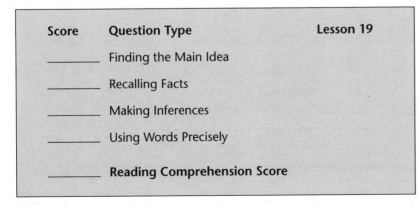

Score	Question Type	Lesson 19
_____	Finding the Main Idea	
_____	Recalling Facts	
_____	Making Inferences	
_____	Using Words Precisely	
_____	**Reading Comprehension Score**	

Author's Approach

Put an X in the box next to the correct answer.

1. The main purpose of the first paragraph is to

☐ a. express an opinion concerning the President's actions.

☐ b. entertain the reader with a pleasant story.

☐ c. make the reader wonder why the President apologized.

2. From the statements below, choose those that you believe the author would agree with.

☐ a. The U.S. government made terrible mistakes as part of the Tuskegee Experiment.

☐ b. The subjects of the Tuskegee Experiment were victims.

☐ c. People who accept free services should not expect to be treated fairly.

3. What does the author imply by saying "Looking back, many people believe that one of the worst aspects of the study was how happy the officials made the men feel"?

☐ a. Some people think it is awful that the officials of the study were so happy.

☐ b. Some people believe that the experiment would have been acceptable if it had made the men feel unhappy.

☐ c. Some people believe that the experiment was particularly disgraceful because it tricked the men into feeling happy while it cruelly abused them.

4. Choose the statement below that best describes the author's position in paragraph 7.

☐ a. The doctors were conducting careful research.

☐ b. The men in the study should have been informed of their condition.

☐ c. The men without syphilis have nothing to complain about.

_____ Number of correct answers

Record your personal assessment of your work on the Critical Thinking Chart on page 198.

2. Choose the best one-sentence paraphrase for the following sentence from the article:

"They [the men] were simply used as human guinea pigs."

☐ a. The men were experimented on without respect, as if they were animals.

☐ b. The men were well taken care of, much as pets are cared for.

☐ c. The study required both humans and guinea pigs.

_____ Number of correct answers

Record your personal assessment of your work on the Critical Thinking Chart on page 198.

Summarizing and Paraphrasing

Put an X in the box next to the correct answer for question 1. Follow the directions provided for the other question.

1. Look for the important ideas and events in paragraphs 5 and 6. Summarize those paragraphs in one or two sentences.

_____

_____

_____

Critical Thinking

Put an X in the box next to the correct answer for questions 1, 2, and 4. Follow the directions provided for the other questions.

1. Which of the following statements from the article is an opinion rather than a fact?

☐ a. "Syphilis attacks the central nervous system."

☐ b. "It was a despicable plan."

☐ c. "They thought the results would show no difference between blacks and whites."

2. From the article, you can predict that if the men had known the real purpose of the experiment, they would

☐ a. still have been willing to become involved in it.

☐ b. never have agreed to be part of it.

☐ c. have demanded that they be paid for their participation.

3. Read paragraph 6. Then choose from the letters below to correctly complete the following statement. Write the letters on the lines.

According to paragraph 6, _____ because _____.

   a.   the recruiters promised free health care, free lunches, and free burial service

   b.   people in rural Alabama were not wealthy

   c.   hundreds of African-American men volunteered for the study

4. What was the cause of death for 28 of the study's subjects?

☐ a.   the withholding of treatment for their syphilis

☐ b.   starvation

☐ c.   poisoning

5. In which paragraph did you find your information or details to answer question 4?

_____

_____ Number of correct answers

Record your personal assessment of your work on the Critical Thinking Chart on page 198.

Personal Response

1. A question I would like answered by the officials who ran the study is

_____

_____

_____

2. I agree with the author because

_____

_____

_____

Self-Assessment

I can't really understand how

_____

_____

_____

THE PSYCHIC WHO WASN'T

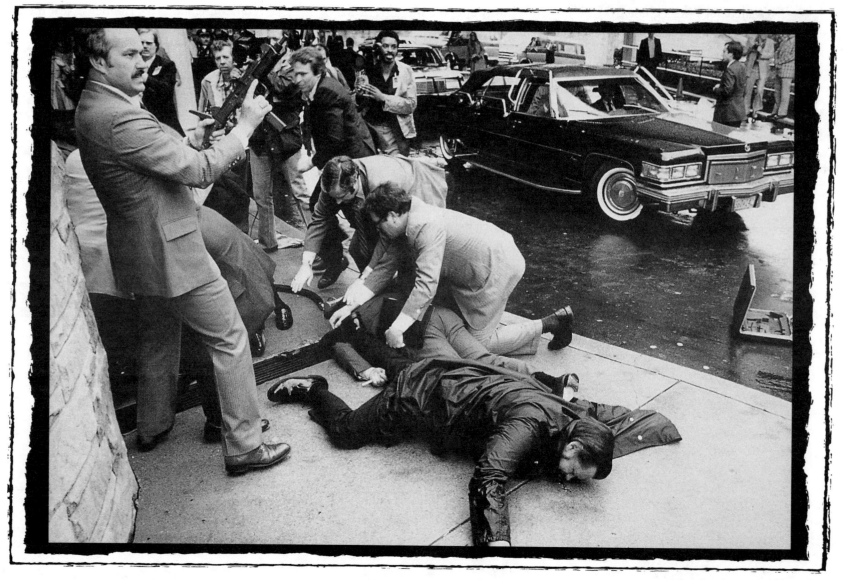

On March 30, 1981, President Ronald Reagan walked out of the Hilton Hotel in Washington, D.C. As he approached his limousine, a gunman took aim at him and fired six quick shots. One bullet struck Reagan between his left ribs. Another severely wounded press secretary James Brady. A police officer and a Secret Service agent were also hit.

2   Reagan was rushed to a nearby hospital. There he underwent two hours of surgery to repair a collapsed lung and other internal damage. The bullet had missed his heart by just three inches.

3   The would-be assassin was a young, sandy-haired man named John Hinckley, Jr. It turned out that Hinckley had acted alone and was not part of a larger conspiracy. He later admitted that he was obsessed with Jodie Foster, the young star of the movie *Taxi Driver*. Hinckley said he identified with Robert De Niro's role from that movie. That character was a taxi driver who tried to assassinate a U.S. senator. Apparently, Hinckley hoped that assassinating the President would impress Jodie Foster.

On March 30, 1981, John Hinckley, Jr., attempted to assassinate President Ronald Reagan outside the Washington Hilton.

4   Shortly after the shooting, it was announced that the whole episode could have been avoided. A 32-year-old Los Angeles psychic named Tamara Rand said she had predicted the entire assassination attempt *three months* before it happened. In fact, she had sent a messenger with a warning to President Reagan. It was, Rand said, received by an unnamed White House aide and ignored.

5   Rand went on to say that she had made her prediction on TV. She'd done it on January 6, 1991, while being interviewed on the *Dick Maurice and Company* talk show. The show had been taped at the studios of Las Vegas television station KTNV.

6   On April 1, Rand called a friend at an NBC station in Los Angeles, saying, "I have a tape of my predictions." She then gave a copy of the tape to that station. On it, Tamara Rand could indeed be seen forecasting the assassination attempt. Her prediction included an image of Reagan getting a "thud" in the chest. She said that the gunman would be a young man with fair hair, acting alone. There would be "shots all over the place." Rand even named the approximate date. "I feel at the end of March, perhaps the last week of March…is a crisis time," she said. She also saw the assassin's name; it was, she said, something like "Jack Humley." Near the end of the tape, Rand said, "I really frankly hope I'm wrong."

7   News of Rand's psychic ability caused a sensation. After all, she had been exactly right on just about everything. The tape of her predictions was picked up by national TV programs. It was shown on April 2 on Cable Network News. It was aired by NBC's *Today* show and ABC's *Good*

Tamara Rand claimed she predicted the assassination attempt.

Morning America. The *Los Angeles Times* also reported the story.

8 What the news media didn't know was that the tape Rand provided had not been made on January 6. Instead, it had been made on March 31, one day after the shooting. That day Rand had returned to KTNV, saying she wanted to tape her predictions again. In her words, she needed to "rearticulate" her January predictions. This was necessary, she told the film crew, because she had slurred and stumbled over a few words on the first tape.

9 The crew didn't think much of it at the time, but when they saw the tape being shown across the country with a January 6 date on it, they realized something fishy was going on. KTNV crew member Forrest Owen said he was "shocked and surprised" when he saw the tape on TV being billed as having been made on January 6. "I know for a fact it wasn't recorded on January 6," said Owen. "I know it was recorded on the 31st of March."

10 Others, too, quickly began to voice their doubts. Arthur Lord, a top NBC official, said, "I have very grave doubts about the authenticity of the tape."

11 The comments of Ed Quinn, the station manager at KTNV, were more pointed. He said, "We have reason to believe the interview was taped on March 31." He then added, "To the best of our knowledge, the Tamara Rand piece [that] aired this morning [April 2]... never aired on KTNV prior to today."

12 By the afternoon of April 2, critics had turned up the heat on both Tamara Rand and Dick Maurice. Rand continued to maintain that she had made her predictions on January 6, and Maurice stood by her. In fact, that same day, Maurice began to sue everyone in sight at KTNV. "I am suing because they are trying to ruin my career," he said. "[Quinn's claim is] totally untrue. It's untrue about a hoax."

13 The very next day, however, ABC and NBC admitted that they hadn't screened the story carefully enough. Jerry Hansen, a producer at the NBC station in Los Angeles said, "It never entered our minds that someone would fabricate something like that. I've been in the business 24 years. I simply believed them."

14 Meanwhile, the evidence of fraud piled up. Maurice had claimed that the original January 6 tape had been erased, but it was found. When reviewers watched it they discovered that Rand had made no mention at all of the shooting. At last, on April 5, Dick Maurice was forced to confess. He had gone along with the hoax, he said, to help boost his friend Rand's career. In an article which appeared in the *Las Vegas Sun*, Maurice wrote, "I am sorry. I've committed a terrible wrong. I have perpetrated a hoax on the public and feel very much ashamed." The next day station KTNV fired him.

15 As for the disgraced Tamara Rand, it seemed that she wasn't much of a psychic after all. If she really could see into the future, she would have known that her little hoax would backfire on her. In the end, all she could do was sob, "I know the people who love me will continue to love me."

If you have been timed while reading this article, enter your reading time below. Then turn to the Words-per-Minute Table on page 195 and look up your reading speed (words per minute). Enter your reading speed on the graph on page 196.

Reading Time: Lesson 20

_____ : _____
Minutes   Seconds

A | Finding the Main Idea

One statement below expresses the main idea of the article. One statement is too general, or too broad. The other statement explains only part of the article; it is too narrow. Label the statements using the following key:

M—Main Idea   **B—Too Broad**   **N—Too Narrow**

_____ 1. Although Tamara Rand tried to deceive the public, her lie was eventually exposed and she was disgraced.

_____ 2. Reports about psychic Tamara Rand's amazing prediction of the shooting of President Reagan aired on CNN, NBC, and ABC.

_____ 3. After President Reagan was shot, so-called psychic Tamara Rand claimed that she had predicted the event, but was later shown to be lying.

_____ Score 15 points for a correct M answer.

_____ Score 5 points for each correct B or N answer.

_____ **Total Score:** Finding the Main Idea

B | Recalling Facts

How well do you remember the facts in the article? Put an X in the box next to the answer that correctly completes each statement about the article.

1. John Hinckley, Jr., shot President Reagan in
   ☐ a. Washington, D.C.
   ☐ b. Chicago, Illinois.
   ☐ c. Pittsburgh, Pennsylvania.

2. Tamara Rand claimed that she had predicted the shooting
   ☐ a. three days before it happened.
   ☐ b. three months before it happened.
   ☐ c. three years before it happened.

3. Rand actually taped the "prediction" on the day
   ☐ a. of the shooting.
   ☐ b. before the shooting.
   ☐ c. after the shooting.

4. When the original tape of the program was found, it proved that
   ☐ a. Rand had not made the prediction.
   ☐ b. Rand had really made the prediction.
   ☐ c. Rand's description of the assassin was just slightly inaccurate.

5. When Rand's friend Maurice was exposed as a liar, he was
   ☐ a. forgiven because he was helping a friend.
   ☐ b. congratulated on a well-done hoax.
   ☐ c. fired from his job.

_____ Score 5 points for each correct answer.

_____ **Total Score:** Recalling Facts

C | Making Inferences

When you combine your own experience and information from a text to draw a conclusion that is not directly stated in that text, you are making an inference. Below are five statements that may or may not be inferences based on information in the article. Label the statements using the following key:

C—Correct Inference   **F—Faulty Inference**

_____ 1. In times of crisis, the large TV networks sometimes place more importance on being the first with the story than on offering the most accurate report.

_____ 2. The movie *Taxi Driver* is to blame for John Hinckley's attack on the President.

_____ 3. It is unlikely that anyone can predict a random future event with total accuracy.

_____ 4. It is not unusual for a performer to retape a TV show in order to improve it.

_____ 5. The events surrounding this hoax proved that Tamara Rand is probably not a psychic.

Score 5 points for each correct answer.

_____ **Total Score:** Making Inferences

D | Using Words Precisely

Each numbered sentence below contains an underlined word or phrase from the article. Following the sentence are three definitions. One definition is closest to the meaning of the underlined word. One definition is opposite or nearly opposite. Label those two definitions using the following key. Do not label the remaining definition.

C—Closest   **O—Opposite or Nearly Opposite**

1. Hinckley said he <u>identified with</u> Robert De Niro's role from that movie.

_____ a. could describe exactly

_____ b. couldn't understand

_____ c. felt a personal connection with

2. In her words, she needed to "<u>rearticulate</u>" her January predictions.

_____ a. say again as clearly as possible

_____ b. recall

_____ c. deny statements said before

3. I have very <u>grave</u> doubts about the authenticity of the tape.

_____ a. serious or significant

_____ b. minor

_____ c. sorrowful

4. The comments of Ed Quinn, the station manager at KTNV, were more <u>pointed</u>.

_____ a. vague and fuzzy

_____ b. to the point; sharp

_____ c. bitter

5. I have <u>perpetrated</u> a hoax on the public and feel very much ashamed.

_____ a. witnessed

_____ b. prevented

_____ c. carried out

_____ Score 3 points for each correct C answer.

_____ Score 2 points for each correct O answer.

_____ **Total Score:** Using Words Precisely

Enter the four total scores in the spaces below, and add them together to find your Reading Comprehension Score. Then record your score on the graph on page 197.

Score	Question Type	Lesson 20
_____	Finding the Main Idea	
_____	Recalling Facts	
_____	Making Inferences	
_____	Using Words Precisely	
_____	**Reading Comprehension Score**	

Author's Approach

Put an X in the box next to the correct answer.

1. What does the author mean by the statement "He [Hinckley] later admitted that he was obsessed with Jodie Foster"?

☐ a. Hinckley said that he hated Jodie Foster and wanted to hurt her somehow.

☐ b. Hinckley said that he was a good friend of Jodie Foster.

☐ c. Hinckley said that he could think of nothing but Jodie Foster and how to get her attention.

2. The main purpose of the first paragraph is to

☐ a. prove that John Hinckley, Jr., was the lone gunman.

☐ b. convey a light-hearted mood.

☐ c. describe the incident that Tamara Rand would later say she had predicted.

3. What does the author imply by saying "critics had turned up the heat on both Tamara Rand and Dick Maurice"?

☐ a. Critics had begun to focus intensely on whether or not Rand and Maurice were telling the truth.

☐ b. Critics began to support Rand and Maurice more strongly.

☐ c. Critics had begun to spread the story of Rand's prediction on Maurice's show.

4. The author tells this story mainly by

☐ a. retelling personal experiences.

☐ b. comparing different topics.

☐ c. describing events in the order they happened.

_____ Number of correct answers

Record your personal assessment of your work on the Critical Thinking Chart on page 198.

Summarizing and Paraphrasing

Follow the directions provided for question 1. Put an X in the box next to the correct answer for the other questions.

1. Look for the important ideas and events in paragraphs 4 and 5. Summarize those paragraphs in one or two sentences.

_____

_____

_____

2. Below are summaries of the article. Choose the summary that says all the most important things about the article but in the fewest words.

☐ a. For a while, Tamara Rand fooled the public into believing she had predicted an 1981 assassination attempt on President Reagan, but later she was exposed as a fraud.

☐ b. Tamara Rand and her friend Dick Maurice were both part of a hoax concerning President Reagan.

☐ c. The major networks and much of the American public were deceived by Tamara Rand and her friend Dick Maurice after an attempt on President Reagan's life in 1981.

3. Read the statement about the article below. Then read the paraphrase of that statement. Choose the reason that best tells why the paraphrase does not say the same thing as the statement.

Statement: Those who viewed the original tape of the January program reported that Rand had made no mention of the shooting that day.

Paraphrase: After seeing the January tape, most people agreed that Rand's prediction of the shooting that day had not been totally accurate.

☐ a. Paraphrase says too much.

☐ b. Paraphrase doesn't say enough.

☐ c. Paraphrase doesn't agree with the statement about the article.

_____ Number of correct answers

Record your personal assessment of your work on the Critical Thinking Chart on page 198.

Critical Thinking

Follow the directions provided for questions 3, 4, and 5. Put an X in the box next to the correct answer for the other questions.

1. Which of the following statements from the article is an opinion rather than a fact?

☐ a. "As for the disgraced Tamara Rand, it seemed that she wasn't much of a psychic after all."

☐ b. "The very next day, however, ABC and NBC admitted that they hadn't screened the story carefully enough."

☐ c. "The bullet had missed his heart by just three inches."

2. From what the article told about Tamara Rand, you can predict that she will

☐ a. sue the networks for telling lies about her.

☐ b. be called upon more often to make predictions of the future.

☐ c. have more difficulty convincing people of her psychic abilities now that she has been caught in a lie.

["\n\n\n\n\n"]

3. Choose from the letters below to correctly complete the following statement. Write the letters on the lines.

In the article, _____ and _____ are alike because they both tried to fool the public.

a. Tamara Rand

b. John Hinckley

c. Dick Maurice

4. Read paragraph 9. Then choose from the letters below to correctly complete the following statement. Write the letters on the lines.

According to paragraph 9, _____ because _____.

a. Rand said that the tape she made on March 31 was made on January 6

b. the TV crew became suspicious that Rand could be perpetrating a hoax

c. Dick Maurice supported his friend Tamara Rand

_____ Number of correct answers

Record your personal assessment of your work on the Critical Thinking Chart on page 198.

Personal Response

1. A question I would like answered by John Hinckley is

_____

_____

_____

2. I wonder why…

_____

_____

_____

_____

Self-Assessment

1. I was confused on question # _____ in section _____

_____ because _____

_____

_____

_____

2. From reading this article, I have learned

_____

_____

_____

_____

THE WAR OF THE WORLDS

AT THIS VERY MOMENT SPACE SHIPS FROM THE BEYOND MAY BE ON THEIR WAY TO DESTROY OUR PLANET!

H.G. WELLS' The War of the Worlds

A poster from the film version of The War of the Worlds

On October 30, 1938, radio listeners in New York and New Jersey tuned in to some lively dance music coming from the Park Plaza Hotel. But a little after 8:00 P.M., the music suddenly stopped. An announcer broke in with an urgent news bulletin: a meteor had just crashed near Grovers Mill, New Jersey. The station then returned to its dance music.

2 A few moments later, the announcer interrupted the show again. "Ladies and gentlemen, I have just been handed a message that came in from Grovers Mill by telephone. Just a moment...." He paused, then delivered the chilling news. "At least 40 people, including six state troopers, lie dead in a field east of the village of Grovers Mill, their bodies burned and distorted beyond all recognition."

3 The announcer went on to say the flaming object that had crashed in Grovers Mill wasn't a meteor at all. It seemed to be some kind of mysterious metal cylinder. The radio station then switched to a reporter at the scene to describe what was happening. "Good heavens, something's wriggling out of the shadow like a grey snake," the reporter

stammered. "Now it's another one and another. They look like tentacles to me. There, I can see the thing's body. It's large as a bear and it glistens like black leather. But that face…it's indescribable."

4 What listeners were hearing was a CBS *Mercury Theatre on the Air* radio play called *The War of the Worlds*. The drama was based on an 1898 book by H. G. Wells with the same title. A 23-year-old theatrical star named Orson Welles directed and starred in the radio show. He thought that on this night before Halloween, a scary show would help spice up people's holiday. And indeed, the show was great entertainment for all those who had tuned in from the beginning. They knew it was make-believe because they had been told it was. As the program started, a standard announcement told listeners that they were about to hear a radio play. Unfortunately, on this evening many listeners tuned in late.

5 Hearing the authentic-sounding "news bulletins," many late listeners assumed the information was true. And as they listened in sheer horror, things in New Jersey got worse, much worse. The slimy creatures oozing out of the shadows were Martians, and they were using a strange and deadly smoke to destroy everything in their path.

6 The radio announcer described the scene as the invaders began to wipe out New York City. "Smoke comes out…black smoke, drifting over the city. People in the streets see it now. They're running towards the East River…thousands of them, dropping like rats. People trying to run away from it, but it's no use. They're falling like flies. Now the smoke's crossing Sixth Avenue…Fifth Avenue…one hundred yards away…it's fifty feet…"

7 Then there was silence, only silence. After a few moments, listeners heard the desperate voice of a ham radio operator searching the airwaves for signs of life. Said the voice, "Isn't there anyone on the air? Isn't there anyone?"

8 By this point in the broadcast, thousands of panic-stricken people had left their radios and were running through the streets shouting, "The world is coming to an end! The world is coming to an end! Prepare to die!" Terrorized listeners in Newark, New Jersey, put wet towels over their faces to protect themselves from the poisonous smoke that they believed was heading their way. One hospital treated 15 people for shock and hysteria. Thousands of other people tried to flee the city in their cars, causing huge traffic jams. Adding to the chaos were unconfirmed reports that people were dying in the panic.

9 Even before the broadcast was over, CBS was flooded with calls from people wanting to know if the program was real. Others called the police and newspapers, asking what they could do to protect themselves. The *New York Times* alone received 875 calls.

Orson Welles during the radio broadcast of H. G. Wells's The War of the Worlds, *1938*

10   Orson Welles could tell that there was trouble brewing. He heard about the frenzied calls flooding the switchboard at CBS. So at the end of the broadcast, he attempted to put listeners at ease. "This is Orson Welles, ladies and gentlemen, out of character to assure you that *The War of the Worlds* has no further significance than as the holiday offering it was intended to be. The Mercury Theatre's own radio version of dressing up in a sheet and jumping out of a bush and saying Boo!"

11   But Welles's words did no good. The people still listening already knew that it was just a scary story. Those who thought it was real didn't stick around long enough to hear the end of the program. They were running wild through the streets.

12   By the next morning, everyone knew the truth. Newspaper headlines on October 31 caught the flavor of the hysteria. The New York *Daily News*, for example, wrote, "FAKE RADIO 'WAR' STIRS TERROR THROUGH U.S.," while the *New York Times* headlined, "RADIO LISTENERS IN PANIC, TAKING WAR DRAMA AS FACT."

13   Many people who had been deceived by the program directed their outrage at CBS and especially at Orson Welles. They had been made to look like fools and they didn't like it. A few even brought lawsuits against CBS, although no one won any damage claims. Despite the widespread panic created by *The War of the Worlds*, no one had died. No one had even been seriously injured.

14   Still, the power of Welles's program could not be denied. The CBS broadcast of the original *The War of the Worlds* has been preserved. And it continues to make for spooky listening on a Halloween night. John Houseman, who worked with Welles on that 1938 program, later said, "To this day, it is impossible to sit in a room and hear the...broadcast, without feeling in the back of your neck some light draft left over from the great wind of terror that swept the nation." 🍃

If you have been timed while reading this article, enter your reading time below. Then turn to the Words-per-Minute Table on page 195 and look up your reading speed (words per minute). Enter your reading speed on the graph on page 196.

Reading Time: Lesson 21

_____ : _____
Minutes   Seconds

A | Finding the Main Idea

One statement below expresses the main idea of the article. One statement is too general, or too broad. The other statement explains only part of the article; it is too narrow. Label the statements using the following key:

M—Main Idea   **B—Too Broad**   **N—Too Narrow**

_____ 1. Public reaction to Orson Welles's radio play, *The War of the Worlds*, proves the power of the media to control people's emotions.

_____ 2. The panic caused by a 1938 radio play was so great that thousands of people tried to flee New York, causing huge traffic jams.

_____ 3. In 1938, when Orson Welles broadcast a terrifying radio play about a Martian invasion, people in New York and New Jersey panicked.

_____ Score 15 points for a correct M answer.

_____ Score 5 points for each correct B or N answer.

_____ **Total Score:** Finding the Main Idea

B | Recalling Facts

How well do you remember the facts in the article? Put an X in the box next to the answer that correctly completes each statement about the article.

1. The first "news report" from Grovers Mill announced that a
    - ☐ a. meteor had fallen.
    - ☐ b. spaceship had landed.
    - ☐ c. war had begun.

2. Orson Welles aired his radio play for the first time on
    - ☐ a. July 4th.
    - ☐ b. Christmas Eve.
    - ☐ c. the night before Halloween.

3. Announcers described the Martian invaders' efforts to wipe out
    - ☐ a. Boston, Massachusetts.
    - ☐ b. New York City.
    - ☐ c. Newark, New Jersey.

4. Listeners wrapped towels around their faces to protect themselves against
    - ☐ a. the light the spaceship was emitting.
    - ☐ b. poisonous smoke.
    - ☐ c. a nuclear blast.

5. Orson Welles wrote and performed the play in order to
    - ☐ a. entertain his listeners.
    - ☐ b. panic his listeners.
    - ☐ c. anger his listeners.

Score 5 points for each correct answer.

_____ **Total Score:** Recalling Facts

C | Making Inferences

When you combine your own experience and information from a text to draw a conclusion that is not directly stated in that text, you are making an inference. Below are five statements that may or may not be inferences based on information in the article. Label the statements using the following key:

C—Correct Inference   F—Faulty Inference

_____ 1. The *Mercury Theatre on the Air* was a popular program that drew thousands of listeners each week.

_____ 2. When people are confused and frightened, they often call the newspaper for information.

_____ 3. In 1938, most people in the New York–New Jersey region were familiar with H.G. Wells's book *The War of the Worlds*.

_____ 4. If you want to be sure that radio listeners hear your message, you should announce it at the beginning of the program.

_____ 5. Almost everyone demands proof before he or she is willing to believe an unlikely story.

Score 5 points for each correct answer.

_____ **Total Score:** Making Inferences

D | Using Words Precisely

Each numbered sentence below contains an underlined word or phrase from the article. Following the sentence are three definitions. One definition is closest to the meaning of the underlined word. One definition is opposite or nearly opposite. Label those two definitions using the following key. Do not label the remaining definition.

C—Closest   O—Opposite or Nearly Opposite

1. An announcer broke in with an <u>urgent</u> news bulletin: a meteor had just crashed near Grovers Mill, New Jersey.

_____ a. calling for immediate attention

_____ b. late-breaking

_____ c. possibly interesting

2. "At least 40 people…lie dead…their bodies burned and <u>distorted</u> beyond all recognition."

_____ a. returned to original shape

_____ b. twisted out of normal condition

_____ c. flattened

3. "But that face…it's <u>indescribable</u>."

_____ a. easy to explain in words

_____ b. horrible

_____ c. not able to be described

4. One hospital treated 15 people for shock and <u>hysteria</u>.

_____ a. high blood pressure

_____ b. overwhelming fear and panic

_____ c. peacefulness

5. He heard about the <u>frenzied</u> calls flooding the switchboard at CBS.

_____ a. showing wild emotions

_____ b. calm and controlled

_____ c. numerous

_____ Score 3 points for each correct C answer.

_____ Score 2 points for each correct O answer.

_____ **Total Score:** Using Words Precisely

Enter the four total scores in the spaces below, and add them together to find your Reading Comprehension Score. Then record your score on the graph on page 197.

Score	Question Type	Lesson 21
_____	Finding the Main Idea	
_____	Recalling Facts	
_____	Making Inferences	
_____	Using Words Precisely	
_____	**Reading Comprehension Score**	

Author's Approach

Put an X in the box next to the correct answer.

1. What is the author's purpose in writing "The War of the Worlds"?
   - ☐ a. To persuade entertainers never to broadcast frightening stories on the radio
   - ☐ b. To emphasize the similarities between New York and New Jersey
   - ☐ c. To inform the reader about a fascinating, true incident

2. Which of the following statements from the article best describes the reaction of listeners who tuned in from the beginning of the broadcast?
   - ☐ a. "They had been made to look like fools and they didn't like it."
   - ☐ b. "By this point in the broadcast, thousand of panic-stricken people had left their radios and were running through the streets.…"
   - ☐ c. "They knew it was make-believe because they had been told it was."

3. From the statements below, choose those that you believe the author would agree with.
   - ☐ a. Orson Welles was surprised by the public's reaction to his play.
   - ☐ b. People are relatively easy to frighten.
   - ☐ c. People should be ready with emergency plans in case of a real attack from Mars.

4. What does the author imply by saying "The *New York Times* alone received 875 calls"?
   - ☐ a. Other newspapers and organizations probably got calls, too.
   - ☐ b. The *New York Times* is the only newspaper that listeners contacted.
   - ☐ c. The *New York Times* received more calls than anyone else.

_____ Number of correct answers

Record your personal assessment of your work on the Critical Thinking Chart on page 198.

Summarizing and Paraphrasing

Follow the directions provided for questions 1 and 2. Put an X in the box next to the correct answer for the other question.

1. Complete the following one-sentence summary of the article using the lettered phrases from the phrase bank below. Write the letters on the lines.

   Phrase Bank:

   a. one actor's opinion of the play

   b. public reaction to the play

   c. a description of the radio play

   The article about *The War of the Worlds* begins with _____, goes on to explain _____, and ends with _____.

2. Reread paragraph 10 in the article. Below, write a summary of the paragraph in no more than 25 words.

   _____

   _____

   _____

   _____

   Reread your summary and decide whether it covers the important ideas in the paragraph. Next, decide how to shorten the summary to 15 words or less without leaving out any essential information. Write this summary below.

   _____

   _____

3. Choose the sentence that correctly restates the following sentence from the article:

   "A few even brought lawsuits against CBS, although no one won any damage claims."

   ☐ a. The lawsuits that a few people brought against CBS were unsuccessful.

   ☐ b. Some people sued CBS, winning only a few dollars.

   ☐ c. Some people brought lawsuits against CBS, but they did not ask for any money in damages.

   _____ Number of correct answers

   Record your personal assessment of your work on the Critical Thinking Chart on page 198.

Critical Thinking

Put an X in the box next to the correct answer for questions 1, 2, 4, and 5. Follow the directions provided for question 3.

1. Which of the following statements from the article is a fact rather than an opinion?

   ☐ a. "One hospital treated 15 people for shock and hysteria."

   ☐ b. "But that face...it's indescribable."

   ☐ c. "To this day, it is impossible to...hear the...broadcast, without feeling in the back of your neck some light draft left over from the...terror that swept the nation."

CRITICAL THINKING

2. From what the article told about the public reaction to the frightening radio play, you can predict that the next time a play like this airs on the radio or TV,

☐ a. listeners will be informed that it is make-believe several times throughout the broadcast.

☐ b. broadcasters will try to fool the public again.

☐ c. no listeners will be deceived by the story.

3. Choose from the letters below to correctly complete the following statement. Write the letters on the lines.

On the positive side, _____, but on the negative side _____.

a. *The War of the Worlds* was written and performed so well that many people believed it

b. *The War of the Worlds* caused wide-spread panic

c. *The War of the Worlds* was aired on the night before Halloween

4. What was the effect of tuning in late to the Halloween production of *The War of the Worlds*?

☐ a. Because they missed the introduction, listeners enjoyed the show more.

☐ b. Because they missed the introduction, listeners became confused and turned their radios off.

☐ c. Because they missed the introduction, listeners thought the invasion was real and panicked.

5. What did you have to do to answer question 3?

☐ a. find an effect (something that happened as a result of another event)

☐ b. find a description (how something looks)

☐ c. draw a conclusion (a sensible statement based on the text and your experience)

_____ Number of correct answers

Record your personal assessment of your work on the Critical Thinking Chart on page 198.

Personal Response

What would you have done if you had been listening to your radio on the night before Halloween, 1938, and heard that New York City had been invaded by creatures from outer space?

_____

_____

_____

Self-Assessment

One of the things I did best when reading this article was

_____

_____

I believe I did this well because

_____

_____

CRITICAL THINKING

Compare and Contrast

Think about the articles you read in Unit Three. Choose the three from which you learned the most. Write the titles of those articles in the first column of the chart below. Use information you learned from the articles to fill in the empty boxes in the chart.

Title	In which profession or walk of life did this deception take place?	How was the deception finally uncovered?	What special skills did the deceiver have that made his or her trickery work for a while?

Most of the deceptions you read about in this unit were uncovered by careful investigators. What personal qualities do you think make a successful investigator? On the lines, list at least three characteristics of such a person and explain why each characteristic is so important. _____

_____

_____

Words-per-Minute Table

Unit Three

Directions: If you were timed while reading an article, refer to the Reading Time you recorded in the box at the end of the article. Use this words-per-minute table to determine your reading speed for that article. Then plot your reading speed on the graph on page 196.

Lesson No. of Words	15 1460	16 1115	17 1240	18 1051	19 1336	20 1091	21 1131	
1:30	842	718	847	733	666	677	681	**90**
1:40	758	646	762	660	599	609	613	**100**
1:50	689	587	693	600	545	554	557	**110**
2:00	632	539	635	550	500	508	511	**120**
2:10	583	497	586	508	461	468	471	**130**
2:20	541	462	544	471	428	435	438	**140**
2:30	505	431	508	440	400	406	408	**150**
2:40	474	404	476	413	375	381	383	**160**
2:50	446	380	448	388	353	358	360	**170**
3:00	421	359	423	367	333	338	340	**180**
3:10	399	340	401	347	315	321	322	**190**
3:20	379	323	381	330	300	305	306	**200**
3:30	361	308	363	314	285	290	292	**210**
3:40	344	294	346	300	272	277	278	**220**
3:50	329	281	331	287	261	265	266	**230**
4:00	316	269	318	275	250	254	255	**240**
4:10	303	258	305	264	240	244	245	**250**
4:20	291	249	293	254	231	234	236	**260**
4:30	281	239	282	244	222	226	227	**270**
4:40	271	231	272	236	214	218	219	**280**
4:50	261	223	263	228	207	210	211	**290**
5:00	253	215	254	220	200	203	204	**300**
5:10	244	208	246	213	193	196	198	**310**
5:20	237	202	238	206	187	190	191	**320**
5:30	230	196	231	200	182	185	186	**330**
5:40	223	190	224	194	176	179	180	**340**
5:50	217	185	218	189	171	174	175	**350**
6:00	211	180	212	183	167	169	170	**360**
6:10	205	175	206	178	162	165	166	**370**
6:20	199	170	201	174	158	160	161	**380**
6:30	194	166	195	169	154	156	157	**390**
6:40	189	162	191	165	150	152	153	**400**
6:50	185	158	186	161	146	149	149	**410**
7:00	180	154	181	157	143	145	146	**420**
7:10	176	150	177	153	139	142	142	**430**
7:20	172	147	173	150	136	138	139	**440**
7:30	168	144	169	147	133	135	136	**450**
7:40	165	140	166	143	130	132	133	**460**
7:50	161	137	162	140	128	130	130	**470**
8:00	158	135	159	138	125	127	128	**480**

Minutes and Seconds | *Seconds*

Plotting Your Progress: Reading Speed

Unit Three

Directions: If you were timed while reading an article, write your words-per-minute rate for that in the box under the number of the lesson. Then plot your reading speed on the graph by putting a small X on the line directly above the number of the lesson, across from the number of words per minute you read. As you mark your speed for each lesson, graph your progress by drawing a line to connect the X's.

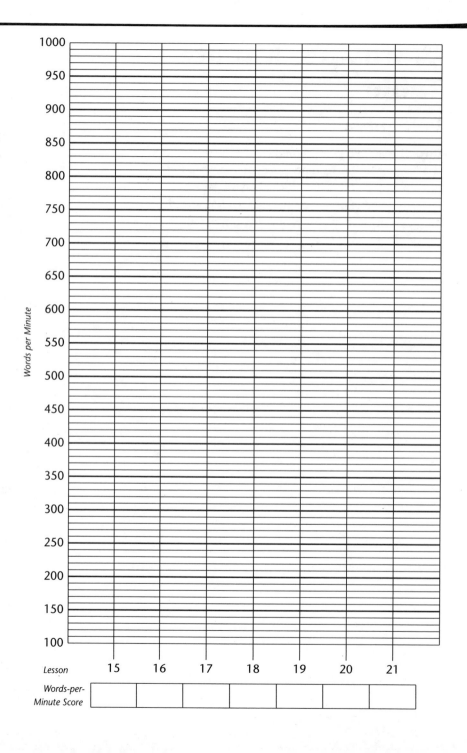

Words per Minute

Lesson	15	16	17	18	19	20	21
Words-per-Minute Score							

Plotting Your Progress: Reading Comprehension

Unit Three

Directions: Write your Reading Comprehension score for each lesson in the box under the number of the lesson. Then plot your score on the graph by putting a small X on the line directly above the number of the lesson and across from the score you earned. As you mark your score for each lesson, graph your progress by drawing a line to connect the X's.

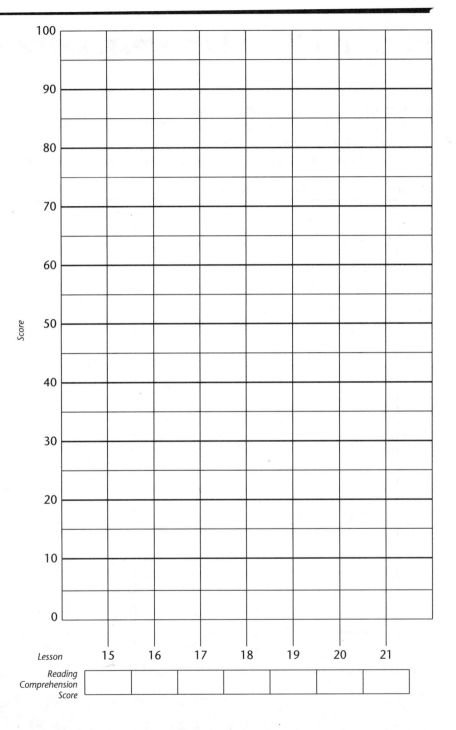

Score

Lesson | 15 | 16 | 17 | 18 | 19 | 20 | 21

Reading Comprehension Score

Plotting Your Progress: Critical Thinking

Unit Three

Directions: Work with your teacher to evaluate your responses to the Critical Thinking questions for each lesson. Then fill in the appropriate spaces in the chart below. For each lesson and each type of Critical Thinking question, do the following: Mark a minus sign (–) in the box to indicate areas in which you feel you could improve. Mark a plus sign (+) to indicate areas in which you feel you did well. Mark a minus-slash-plus sign (–/+) to indicate areas in which you had mixed success. Then write any comments you have about your performance, including ideas for improvement.

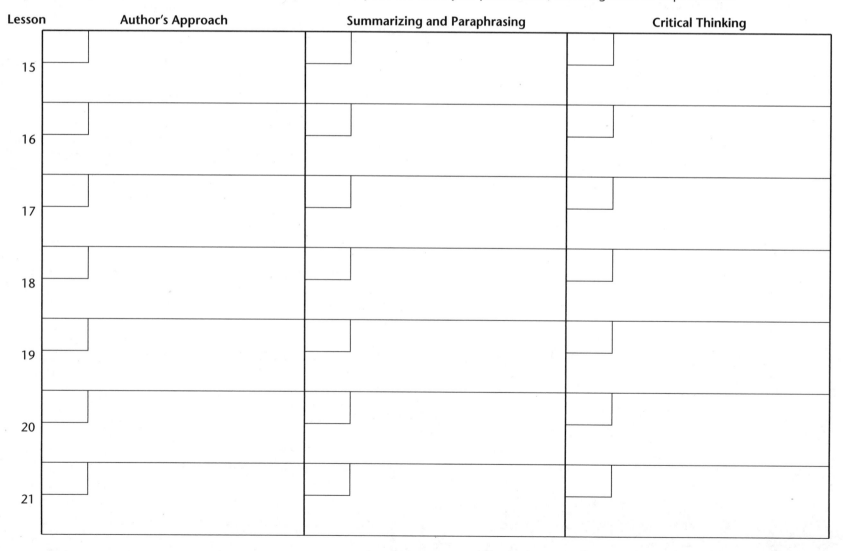

Lesson	Author's Approach	Summarizing and Paraphrasing	Critical Thinking
15			
16			
17			
18			
19			
20			
21			

Picture Credits